My Own Identity:

An Introduction to Self-Discovery

Marcela Melnic

My Own Identity: An Introduction to Self-Discovery
by Marcela Melnic

ISBN 979-8-9853763-2-6

Copyright © 2023 Institute for Education, Research, and Scholarships

All rights reserved. This work may not be translated or copied in whole or in part without the written permission of the copyright holder except for brief excerpts in connection with reviews or scholarly analysis. Use in connection with any form of information storage and retrieval, electronic adaptation, computer software, or by similar or dissimilar methodology now known or hereafter developed is forbidden.

The use in this publication of trade names, trademarks, service marks, and similar terms, even if they are not identified as such, is not to be taken as an expression of opinion as to whether or not they are subject to proprietary rights. References to various copyrighted trademarks, characters, marks and registered marks may appear in this book. Rather than use a trademark symbol with every occurrence of a trademarked name, logo, or image we use the names, logos, and images only in an editorial fashion with no intention of infringement of the trademark.

Cover Photo: Marcela Melnic by Heidi Browne.

Table of Contents

Preface 5
Chapter 1: Make sense of your past... 17
Chapter 2: Destiny and relationships 27
Chapter 3: Personality traits.. 39
Chapter 4: The self-healing 48
Chapter 5: Happiness is a direction to self-realization 59
Chapter 6: Don't lose yourself in someone else's dream 71
Chapter 7: Set up healthy boundaries 83
Chapter 8: Beliefs and values shape our identity........................ 91
Chapter 9: Become your best self... 103
Chapter 10: Reaching your greatest potential........................... 112
Chapter 11: Have clear goals 127
Chapter 12: Have faith in your capabilities 135
Chapter 13: Things you don't know about yourself................... 141
Chapter 14: Plan for your future self 148
Acknowledgments 155
Bibliography 156

Marcela Melnic

My Own Identity: An Introduction to Self-Discovery

Preface

"The value of identity of course is so often with purpose."
— Richard Grant

I believe it is important to reflect on one's national and cultural identity to better understand the differences among people from various nations. History has taught us that culture is constantly evolving due to internal and external influences and even our own cultures and values change over time. In today's interconnected world, people from different nations and cultures are growing closer due to economic and political reasons. As cultures converge, effective communication becomes the most important skill for anyone wishing to thrive in international society. The history of communication and the relationships formed during the early stages of global communication still reverberate in the interactions between nations today. While many aspects of individual cultures and values have indeed evolved, understanding modern communication requires studying the communications of the past.

Do our experiences shape who we are? Are the memories we retain from these experiences more impactful in shaping our identity than the experiences themselves? Moreover, if our memories and experiences indeed influence who we are, how can one person justify judging another when they are unaware of all the experiences and memories that have shaped them? Many individuals believe that our experiences do shape who we are, and they consider memories of those experiences to be equally important. On the other hand, some individuals believe in a core identity that remains unchanged, a fundamental essence of one's existence. I believe that we are defined by our experiences, and I do not believe in any fixed "core" idea that defines our identity. Ever since I was young, I have pondered the notion that my identity is simply the culmination of my experiences. This thought has always simultaneously terrified and liberated me.

Every experience we have shapes who we are in one way or another, every single one, no matter how seemingly insignificant. Even a small experience can lead to changes within us. An unimportant moment may influence our emotions on a particular day, setting off a chain reaction that affects our actions and, ultimately, impacts our entire life. Our identity is merely a collection of moments and events that shape our lives.

For instance, throughout my life, numerous experiences have contributed to shaping the person I am today. During my middle childhood, my life mostly revolved around playing and having fun. At that stage, I did not put much effort into various areas or work hard to achieve specific goals. However, as time passed, my life experiences began to have a profound effect on me, molding the person I am today.

My life underwent significant changes during early childhood. It was a time when I began to observe and comprehend the impacts that affected my family.

Although I understood these changes better later in life, let me start with the first significant impact that began around the time of my birth and continued thereafter. It all started with the dissolution of the Soviet Union (1988-1991), which led to the Republic of Moldova becoming an independent country. These changes had a far-reaching effect, not just on my family but on the entire nation. The process involved internal political, economic, and ethical disintegration within the USSR. From 23rd May 1991 until the declaration of independence on 27th August 1991, it was renamed the Republic of Moldova while remaining a constituent republic of the USSR. Moldova's independence was officially recognized on 26th December of the year the USSR dissolved. Geographically, Moldova is bordered by Romania to the west and Ukraine to the north, east, and south. Since gaining independence in 1991, Moldova has faced a myriad of challenges, originating from four problematic situations. First, the country has endeavored to establish a viable state where no tradition of self-government and sovereignty previously existed. Secondly, lacking a local political tradition, Moldova faced difficulties in reaching a consensus on a constitution and finding political leaders untainted by associations with the highly centralized, authoritarian Soviet Union. Thirdly, the transition from a controlled economy to a free-market economy has been turbulent. Under Soviet rule, Moldova had a predominantly agricultural economy, centered around state and collective farms. After gaining independence, many of these farms were disbanded and handed over to individuals. However, this led to significant dislocation, productivity losses, and allegations of corruption. The economic transition was further hindered by the fact that much of Moldova's industry was located in the separatist region of Transnistria, which declared independence from Moldova in 1991, resulting in a brief civil war. Although a cease-fire was declared in 1992, tensions persisted between Moldova and Transnistria. Moreover, Transnistria is also the source of Moldova's electricity, which has been cut off at various times. As a result, Moldova's path to nationhood has been fraught with challenges, from the initial efforts at nation-building to the country's ongoing pursuit of peace and prosperity in the 21st century.

During the Russian imperial and Soviet periods, the Moldovan language (as it was then called) was written in the Cyrillic alphabet. Soviet scholars, mainly for political reasons, insisted that this language was an independent Romance language distinct from Daco-Romanian. However, in reality, Daco-Romanian and Moldovan are virtually identical, with differences limited to phonetics and vocabulary. In 1989, the script of the Moldovan language was changed to the Latin alphabet, sparking a heated debate over whether the language should be called Romanian or Moldovan. By the middle of the first decade of the 21st century, both sides reached a general agreement that Moldovan and Romanian were, in fact, the same language. This meant that the entire population had to adjust and learn the new alphabet. Additionally, they had to adapt to the new currency, changing from the ruble to the leu, which originates from a Romanian word meaning "lion". These changes affected everyone in the country, and every family had to cope with multiple adjustments simultaneously.

As a result, I realized early in life that political identity has a powerful influence on an individual's attitudes and beliefs, which, in turn, can impact their behavior and shape who they may become. Similarly, firsthand experiences with an issue can also influence attitudes and beliefs, exerting a significant impact on self-reports of emotional distress, threat perception, discomfort with exposure, support for restrictions, and perception of under/overreaction by individuals and institutions, all of which contribute to shaping our identity.

I learned early in life that change is inevitable. Whether we plan for it or not, life is constantly in a state of flux. Instead of hiding from it, we should embrace it. Becoming comfortable with change and accepting its inevitability helps prepare oneself for life's unexpected curveballs, moments of excitement, and tragedies that are unavoidable over a lifetime.

As humans, we process beautiful aspects, but we must acknowledge certain characteristics: we all experience breakdowns, have moments of weakness, and have areas to grow and improve upon. Keeping this in mind while dealing with challenging situations, whether within our families, countries, or any other relationships, is crucial. The key is to understand and work together to move forward and make peace with the past.

Life doesn't always go according to plan, and unfortunately, some things are beyond our control. Instead of fighting it, accept it, knowing it's all part of the Universe's plan for you, and no matter what, you will grow from it. When you go through something traumatic, it teaches you not to fuss over the little things. It's not always easy when faced with an issue (big or small), but being aware that the situation will pass and won't significantly affect you in an hour, a day, or even a year, helps you not to sweat too much! Even when the world seems to be crashing down, know that you have the strength to get through it and stand back up again.

My Own Identity: An Introduction to Self-Discovery

Humans are incredibly resilient, and when we tap into our inner strength, we can overcome any hurdle if we stay positive and put our minds to it. During painful moments, just remind yourself of how strong you are. You will get through it!

Going through a family divorce in a country's changing times has, in my opinion, been an automatic ticket to having an open mind. This experience has expanded and stretched my mind for the better. It might sound crazy, but I am genuinely grateful for having gone through these tough times.

Yes, grateful! I firmly believe that this experience has shaped me into the strong, resilient, and well-rounded woman I am today. The pain and changes I've experienced have become the motivation for me to help others find happiness as much as I seek it for myself. As Tony Robbins said: "Your problem is your GIFT." This problem is my gift. It has defined the person I am today and has been the driving force behind why I do what I do. It has given me the passion and fuel to assist others in creating happiness in their lives and helping with what I can in finding themselves when life hits them really hard.

My work for the Institute for Education, Research, and Scholarship based in Los Angeles involves helping students and recent graduates from all over the world find internships or full-time jobs in the U.S. It has created in me the belief that cultural exchange provides an invaluable opportunity to explore other cultures, traditions, customs, beliefs, societies, languages, and much more.

Hence, such opportunities allow us to view the world through a different lens, providing alternative perspectives that broaden our horizons and increase our tendency toward acceptance. The cultural exchange makes us more aware of ourselves and our culture. While increasing knowledge about the world we live in.

Helping others to recognize their greatness is one of the most rewarding experiences I have encountered in my life. I cherish cultural exchange and relish meeting people from all over the world who are brave enough to take the step to come to a new country filled with new ideas. Every day presents something new: a tidbit of information, a discussion of a significant concept (like our "peace" competition), politics, or the values they hold dear. Engaging in cultural exchange teaches us to listen, explore, and compromise. Oh, if only cultural exchange experiences were a requirement for the world's leaders!

A Roman philosopher once said "As the soil, however rich it may be, cannot be productive without cultivation, so the mind without culture can never produce good fruit," I strongly believe that this statement holds more truth than most of us realize. I am still growing into someone with a cultivated mind. Growing up means finding out who you want to be and then working towards becoming that person.

When I was a child struggling with family difficulties, I couldn't figure out for myself who I am, what I want to be, what I can contribute to this world, or how I can be useful to others. It was challenging for me to understand my abilities and the person I aspired to become. However, in my late 20's, I discovered my capabilities and found my path. After living in New York City for a few years, I was exposed to cultural exchange from different cultural backgrounds, and I came to the realization that I enjoy meeting new people from different places, with different ways of thinking, living, and cultural backgrounds.

What I have learned the most is that our culture and influences from other cultures often determine who we are. Here in New York City, I have probably done more growing up than I did throughout high school, mainly because of this exact reason. After graduating high school, I knew I was not yet ready to face the world as an adult capable of taking care of myself, especially with all the emotional challenges life had to offer. I wanted to break free from my sheltered life and experience the world. I aimed to expand my knowledge of people and become worldly wise. That's why I joined the work I do today, as I knew it would take me outside of my comfort zone, allowing me to learn and cherish experiences beyond my imagination.

When I came to New York City in my early 20s, I learned that American culture encourages pride, patriotism, independence, and a go-big attitude in everything. Americans are unafraid to voice their beliefs and fight for what they want. Living among New Yorkers, I have learned to embrace who I am without worrying about others' opinions. I have witnessed how effortlessly New Yorkers choose their style and appearance, something that was not easy to do where I come from.

Back in my hometown, we grew up wearing school uniforms that came with a very strict dress code. This dress code was deeply ingrained in our culture, making it difficult for us to deviate from it. However, being here in New York City, I have come to realize how liberating it is to choose and express yourself in a way that feels comfortable and authentic.

On the 4th of July, I experienced a surge of national pride and unity that brought tears to my eyes. It was amazing to see how Americans stand attentively while singing their national anthem, displaying their pride, a cultural trait that defines America today. On Halloween, I was astounded by the grandiosity with which Americans celebrate, from elaborate decorations to abundant candy and enthusiastic trick-or-treating. Americans certainly know how to go big, showcasing their boundless enthusiasm. On Thanksgiving, I was touched by the love, care, and festivity displayed by the American people, embodying the beautiful traditions I had previously only seen in movies.

During my time in New York, I have encountered diverse approaches to handling things from all around the world. This exposure has allowed me to cherry-pick and blend various methods, broadening my perspective and enabling me to form well-thought-out conclusions on crucial life matters, thanks to the multitude of opinions I've heard.

Thanks to the cultural exchange I have experienced, I am well on my way to becoming a well-rounded individual with better-formulated opinions. I cannot begin to express my gratitude to everyone I've met throughout this entire journey. The diverse experiences I have lived through, including my traumas, have allowed me to gain a deeper understanding of myself and how the world operates.

This transformative experience has changed me into a progressive individual, whose mind is now fertile ground for new ideas. I aspire to work for an organization that empowers others to have similar eye-opening experiences. My heart swells with fondness for the impact this has had on me. Every experience, after all, shapes who we are in one way or another.

There's a prevailing belief that many people unquestioningly accept their identity. This belief suggests that there exists a core "you," and as you journey through life, you acquire memories, beliefs, and experiences. While these memories and beliefs contribute to who you are, they are only parts of the larger whole of your core identity. This concept often becomes an excuse for both who people are and who they have become, leading to potential complications. The idea of core identity traces back to the 1st-century philosopher Plato, who posited that we essentially consist of a simple, immaterial soul, a notion that laid the groundwork for this concept. Over time, debates emerged around the topic of understanding one's own identity.

One of the early challengers to this idea was the philosopher Locke, who proposed that individuals should take responsibility for their actions. Consequently, Locke began connecting personal identity to moral responsibility—an approach that aligns with my aim when I ask questions like, "If we are a culmination of our experiences and memories, how can we justify judging others without knowing all of their experienced and memories?"

Now, not everyone embraced Locke's idea of identity. Joseph Butler, in particular, questioned Locke's perspective as he remained steadfast in his belief in Plato's substance-based identity. Butler regarded Locke's stance as a "wonderful mistake." According to Butler, "While memory can reveal my identity with some experience, it does not make that experience me."

Butler emphasized, "What I am remembering are the experiences of a substance, namely, the substance that constitutes me now." Thus both Butler and Pluto adhered to the concept of a core self, while Locke stood as a lone ranger, believing that our identity is shaped by our experiences and memories.

Locke and Reid raise a challenge against Butler by questioning how an unchanging identity can be formed through experiences and memories that are forever changing. Both Butler and Reid rejected Locke's perspective on identity and instead adopted a substance-based view. However, I believe that Butler and Reid's arguments against Locke's view have several flaws. For example, they challenge Locke's idea by arguing that identity persists even through the loss of memory, suggesting that one wouldn't cease to exist after experiencing amnesia. While this argument seems plausible, there's an alternative perspective to consider. One might have direct memories of a past self, which itself had direct memories of an earlier self, forming a chain of overlapping direct memories throughout life. However, this chain only holds if we assume that memories have only faded and not vanished entirely. What if the memories are completely gone? Even then, Locke's theory remains strong because the experiences and memories we once had left us with beliefs, desires, goals, and intentions. Even when the memory of those experiences is lost, the impact they had on us remains ingrained subconsciously. Isn't that interesting?

We are left with beliefs, goals, intentions, and desires; we may not remember where we got them, but we have them, and this avoids the objections of Reid and Butler, strengthening Locke's theory. Another theory that challenges Reid and Butler's argument comes from Chad and Robert of NPR'S Radiolab. They proposed that the safest, most genuine, and honest memories are memories held by people who can't remember. Therefore, when you lose your memory, you might become more authentically yourself than ever before. Robert also agrees with the notion that we are shaped by our memories and experiences.

He says, "Really what I am is a string of memories, that's the closest way of describing the real me as I can find. I own those memories, and they define me." Philosopher Julian Baggini also believes in this theory and states, "It is a shift from thinking of yourself as a thing that has all of the experiences." He uses a metaphor that I find perfectly elucidates this theory: Think of a watch. A watch comprises parts— the chain, the face, and the hands, and these parts together make up the watch, but there is no essence of the watch that possesses these parts. The watch is simply a collection of these parts. Baggini asserts, "We are a process. It's fluid, it's forever changing." Twentieth-century philosopher Jean-Paul Sartre holds a similar view of self-identity. He believes we are not a self, but a presence-to-self. In doing so, Sartre challenges the beliefs of Plato, Butler, and Reid regarding a core identity within each of us. He argues that there is no such thing as a core. Sartre states, "Freedom is the definition of man" and we understand that freedom brings responsibility. This ties back into what I mentioned earlier. The idea that there is no core identity places the responsibility for who we are and who we become on each of us. As Satre says, "We are responsible for our "world" as the horizon of meaning in which we operate, and thus, everything in it, so far as their meaning and value are assigned by our life-orienting fundamental "choice." Sartre believes that this fundamental "choice" forms the basis for our subsequent decisions. This aligns with my perspective, and it's why the moment I was able to choose to come to New York City in my early 20s felt so liberating to me.

I was choosing my own experiences, fully aware that this decision would influence all subsequent choices and shape my future experiences. By extension, it would permanently alter my identity and determine who I would become. The power to take control of our own identity and life is profound and should not be disregarded due to the idea of an unchanging core identity.

That idea is entirely ludicrous to me. The idea of a core self feels like an excuse to rationalize our actions. It seems like something we say to justify our behavior and the decisions we make. I strongly believe that we should consider ourselves as beings capable of growth and change.

Daniel Kahneman, a contemporary philosopher, believes that experience and memory play different roles in shaping who we are. He believes in the existence of an "experiencing self who lives in the present and knows the present" and a "remembering self that keeps score and maintains the story of our life." I find this philosophy agreeable. Ultimately, he says, "What we get to keep from our experiences is a story." This idea has established a connection between experience and memory, as they contribute to shaping our identity. Now, there's the issue of comparing ourselves to others and judging others' decisions. If we are a culmination of all of our experiences and memories, and as Sartre states, our fundamental choices form the basis for our subsequent decisions, then it becomes unjustifiable to judge someone else or compare yourself to others. Each individual possesses a completely unique collection of memories and experiences, and we all have reasons for our actions and choices. This philosophy aligns with the famous quote: "Never judge a person until you've walked a mile in their shoes." We can't judge someone because we don't have access to all of their memories and experiences. I strongly believe in the truth of this statement, as I have found myself making uniform judgments about people in the past, only to realize later that I was completely wrong due to my lack of understanding of their backgrounds.

We can never fully comprehend a person's experiences and memories because we cannot be inside another person's mind; therefore, passing judgment on anyone is unjustifiable.

I also understand the pain of being judged without others knowing my memories and experiences; it is a terrible feeling.

When I moved to New York, I was quickly labeled as someone who was not truly "me". People thought they knew me based on the way I looked or acted in the first couple of days. However, they couldn't have known me, and whoever they believed I was, it wasn't the real me.

There's one experience that I repeatedly have, and that is the experience of moving. I am aware that moving frequently has changed how I interact with people and how I perceive friendships. It has had a profound impact on my social connections. I have always been curious about how different I would be if I hadn't lived in certain places, undergone specific experiences, and met certain individuals. With my frequent moves, I have had the opportunity to meet numerous people. I firmly believe that everyone we truly know, and have meaningful connections with, changes us in some way or another. After all, a relationship is an experience in itself. This is why relationships hold such importance. They not only teach us about society but also provide valuable insights into ourselves. Without relationships, there would be limited opportunities for personal growth.

Overall, I strongly believe that experiences and memories play a significant role in shaping who we are. An experience can lead to a belief, desire, or goal, while a memory can leave us with intentions. All of these aspects contribute to defining our identity, and they are never fully lost. Even when we can no longer remember, the memory still resides deep within our minds. Therefore, I agree with Locke's philosophy that we are a product of all our experiences and memories. When we embrace the mindset that we are in control of who we are and who we become, we foster an essential aspect of progress. We take responsibility for our actions instead of attributing them to an unchanging core identity. With this sense of empowerment, there are no limits to the positive changes we can make within ourselves, our communities, and our world. Keeping this in mind, I discovered my passion and my true identity. Everybody not to give up, not to give in. There is always an answer to everything.

My Own Identity: An Introduction to Self-Discovery

Chapter 1: Make sense of your past

"The past can't hurt you anymore, not unless you let it."
— Alan Moore

I believe that most people's identity is rooted in their identities; in what they align themselves with. What a person associates themselves with ultimately defines who they are, as all aspects of identity are interconnected with something else. For instance, a Moldovan person identifies as Moldovan, and this becomes an integral part of their identity. Similarly, the same person may identify as male or female, a member of a particular religious group, a brother or sister, a child, an employee, and so on. On a more personal level, they might identify as a loser, feeling helpless to influence the course of their lives, or as someone who is compelled to hate a particular religious group simply because that is what members of their religious group are "supposed" to do. Although such personal beliefs may lack a basis in reality, they are often unquestioningly accepted by those who hold them. Consequently, these people act upon their mistaken or irrational beliefs, leading to self-created problems and issues in their surroundings.

Identity is not solely about what you know; it also encompasses how you perceive and understand the world. People are not born with a fully developed identity; rather, it is something that evolves. In the early stages of life, young children have simple identities and tend to see things in a straightforward and generally self-serving manner. An interesting example of this can be found in Moldova, where a common expression is used, which might seem a bit peculiar at first - "7 ani de acasa," literally translating to "seven years at home."

What does it mean? Even today, a child is not legally required to attend a full-time school until the age of seven. During this time, the child is expected to be at home, learning how to behave properly. Essentially, anything that one might later scold them for not doing "correctly" is what they were supposed to have learned during those seven years of manners, politeness, decorum, and "proper" behavior. Therefore, saying someone doesn't have "7 ani de acasa" is equivalent to saying they're rude, ill-mannered, and poor upbringing as a child. The phrase "7 ani de acasa" signifies having learned "proper behavior," and anyone rude or uncouth supposedly lacks the proper training or scolding that a child should have received at home. When it comes to child development, it has been said that the most crucial milestones in a kid's life occur by the age of seven. The philosopher Aristotle once said, "Give me a child until he is seven, and I will show you the man." With these facts in mind, we must wonder if any recent research supports Aristotle's hypothesis. While providing a safe environment for children is essential, imperfect conditions such as early trauma, illness, or injury don't necessarily determine our kid's entire well-being. The first seven years of life may not hold absolute significance, but studies do show that this period plays an important role in a child's development of social skills.

As people grow older and wiser, they identify themselves with other people, places, and things in increasingly sophisticated ways, moving away from their initial selfishness. For instance, a young child may see their mother as someone who exists solely to take care of them, but as they grow older, they begin to appreciate that their mother has needs of her own. Consequently, they act less selfishly towards her and take her and consider her needs. However, sometimes life events interrupt this natural progression from selfishness to thoughtfulness, causing people's identities to stop evolving. These people may be chronologically adults but continue to relate to others in a selfish manner, characteristic of a younger child. This clash of self-expectations with those of others can create problems for both themselves and those around them, as people expect a more adult, responsive, and responsible identity to be present. Whether due to mistaken beliefs or development delays, identity problems can lead people to struggle with adopting perspective towards other important life tasks, resulting in a wide range of life problems.

My Own Identity: An Introduction to Self-Discovery

Developing a sense of self or identity is an essential part of each individual's maturation process. Struggling with various aspects of identity is natural and normal. It takes time and may be challenging to develop an identity or a sense of self, along with the desired traits one wants to embody. Without a strong sense of self or when struggling with identity issues, we may experience anxiety and insecurity. Some individuals may find themselves struggling with identity issues, which can lead to depression, hopelessness, addiction, and more. Psychotherapy offers a place for people to discuss issues related to their identity. Through psychotherapy, people can work towards reducing their depression, finding effective coping strategies for the challenges associated with their identity issues, and ultimately embark on a journey of self-discovery.

That's a journey, and the most important adventure of our lives is discovering who we really are. However, many of us wander through life without knowing ourselves, influenced by an unrelenting inner critic that feeds us misconceptions about who we are. We mistakenly regard self-understanding as self-indulgence, and as a result, we continue without asking ourselves the most important question we'll ever ask: Who am I? How can I find my true self? What are my capabilities? What values can I bring to this world? What does it mean to find oneself? As Mary Oliver eloquently put it, "What is it you plan to do with your one wild and precious life?"

Finding yourself may sound like an inherently self-centered goal, but it is an unselfish process that forms the foundation of everything we do in life. To become the most valuable person to the world around us, the best partner, parent, etc., we must know who we are, what we value, and what we have to offer. This personal journey is one that every individual will benefit from taking. It involves a process of breaking down, shedding layers that no longer serve us and don't reflect our true selves. Yet, it also entails a tremendous act of building up, recognizing who we aspire to be, and passionately pursuing our unique destiny. It's a matter of embracing our power while remaining open and vulnerable to our experiences.

First and foremost, recognize that it is your life, not someone else's. The initial step in making sense of your life is understanding that you are in control of how you live it. Many times, we encounter problems when we try to live our lives based on other people's expectations. Your success or failure should be entirely your business, not someone else's, and the effort or lack of effort you put into achieving what you want should be under your control. Remember that we all have only one life to live; therefore, make it count and worthwhile, while you still can.

The world is filled with many things we wish didn't exist. Nevertheless, we have no choice but to find ways to coexist with these challenges. Amidst all that is happening today, it is important to prioritize what matters most to you and direct your attention solely toward those things. Prioritize your values. Consider if you care about love for your fellow man, equality, fairness, equity, peaceful coexistence, and more. Identify what matters most to you through self-evaluation, and focus on those aspects you deeply care about. Set concrete and achievable goals for yourself.

There is a saying that, "He who fails to plan, plans to fail." Amid all the noise and confusion, you should be able to decide and set your own life goals. What are your aspirations? What are your dreams? And what do you need to do to move from point A to point B? Remember that your goals should be tailored to fit your particular situation, as what might work for me may not work for you. While setting up your goals, ensure they are realistic, achievable, time-bound, and open to evaluation, allowing for changes or updates when necessary. Once you have outlined and specified your goals, start taking the necessary steps no matter how small, to reach your desired destination. Focus on the things you have control over. There are certain aspects of life that we have no control over, such as the parents who gave birth to us, our ancestry, genealogy, or even the weather outside. Why bother worrying about those things?

Instead of wasting time on uncontrollable factors, why not concentrate on what you can control, like your educational status, career choice, and where to live, among others?

Consciously make the effort to live a positive life with an attitude of joy. I must tell you that whether you like to accept it or not, there will be times when life feels like a complete waste of time or a total bore altogether. There will be events that leave you questioning "why" endlessly. People whom you thought loved you and cared for you might betray you, making you feel like you want to lose your mind. Some may even insult and malign you. But when these situations arise, what should you do? It is important to realize that such things do happen, and they might happen to you. However, do not lose your cool or succumb to life's pressures, wishing to disappear. Instead, maintain a positive attitude at all times, so that when these challenges arise, you can simply shrug your shoulders and say, "It's one of those things. Let's focus on the solution instead of the problem."

An interesting fact that I have recently learned is that triggers have deep roots in our past. For example, a sentence, an image, or a distressing memory can act as a trigger. Our brain tends to take shortcuts, assuming that if it has experienced something similar before, the new experience will be just the old one, evoking the same feelings and thoughts we had the first time around. The brain is trying to help us by saying: "I've been through this before, I know what to expect, and I've got this." Consequently, we respond to the new situation based on our past experiences before analyzing it thoroughly.

As children, we cannot often discern what's true or not, and we tend to believe what we are told. For instance, if I was bullied and told that I'm not as good as others, that I am stupid, or that I am responsible for my parent's divorce, these misconceptions (which they truly are!) can continue to affect me throughout my life. They can resurface automatically beyond my conscious control, causing distress and creating problems.

All of my experiences while growing up, including my thoughts, images, and feeling, were stored in my brain. As these accumulated, they shaped how I view the world, and how I interpret and make sense of things. Many of these memories might be outside my awareness, but they are stored nonetheless and can resurface when triggered. Consequently, these memories can make me feel unworthy when I am not or scared even when my conscious mind knows I will be OK. Instead of responding to the present moment, I might react based on a distressing event I witnessed 20 years ago. This memory system can be activated at any time, leading to reactions ranging from mild to intense, leaving me wondering why I might have overreacted to a situation without any apparent reason.

So, why does this happen? How are these memories different from everyday memories? Apologies in advance, as I'm not a brain expert, but I'll do my best to describe it based on the research and books I've read!

Trauma memories are different from everyday memories. They can surface in various examples, as I mentioned earlier, but they can also manifest in more extreme forms, as you might have read about in people with Post-Traumatic Stress Disorder (PTSD). For instance, a veteran might drop to the floor when a car backfires, believing they are back in a war zone. In everyday memories, we are aware that they occurred in the past and that they are not happening in the present. However, in the case of trauma memories, it can feel as though the event is happening right now, blurring the sense of time.

I'm sure all of you are aware of the fight-flight response, right? This response originates from our cave-dwelling days when survival was paramount. It's a part of our brain that functions as a threat protection system, often referred to as the fight-flight system. This system is responsible for primitive instincts needed for survival, such as seeking warmth, food, avoiding threats, and mating. When we identify a threat (e.g., a trauma), our threat system gets activated, making us feel anxious and threat-focused to protect ourselves, just like our ancestors needed to escape from saber-toothed tigers, for example. This system can prompt us to fight (get angry or frustrated), flee (feel scared or powerless), freeze (due to the overwhelming nature of the threat), dissociate (seek to turn away from or forget the trauma), or even experience a combination of these responses!

So, when there is a potential threat, the amygdala acts as the brain's alarm, alerting us to the presence of danger. It triggers bursts of anxiety to prompt action. It responds quickly (due to our survival instincts, reminiscent of facing saber-toothed tigers), but it lacks discernment; in other words, it can be a bit impulsive, not taking the time to consider whether something is genuinely a threat, simply opting for a 'better to be safe than sorry' attitude. Consequently, it activates the sympathetic nervous system, releasing chemicals that trigger the fight-or-flight response in the body. The amygdala is also the repository for emotional and body memories, including traumatic experiences.

The part responsible for this analyzing process is the hippocampus. It records the times and places of events and cross-references them to validate the threats that arise, the hippocampus checks its validity; if it determines that it isn't a real threat, it sends a message to the amygdala, saying 'thanks, but no thanks.' As a result, the amygdala calms down, and we feel less anxious or agitated. On the other hand, when a genuine threat is present, the hippocampus gives the green light for the appropriate response. It then stores the date and time of the threat for future reference, if you know what I mean.

So, as I mentioned earlier, trauma memories differ from everyday memories, and they are also stored in different parts of the brain. Trauma memories are stored in the primitive part of the brain known as the amygdala. When something traumatic happens (e.g., a divorce), the brain can become overwhelmed, and we are not in a relaxed state to process the information properly. As a result, the amygdala blocks the hippocampus, preventing the meaningful encoding of the event, including its time and place. Consequently, the memory does not get properly organized or tagged with contextual details. Hence, the traumatic memory remains stored in the amygdala without a clear sense of time or place, resulting in fragmented and incoherent recollections. This explains why we may only recall bits of the event or struggle to remember it sequentially. Additionally, traumatic memories can be triggered by events that remind you of the trauma, even if this is not conscious and occur involuntarily; they may just pop up, as in the example above with the divorce. Because these memories lack a clear sense of time, we can feel as though the traumatic event is happening in the present and respond as we did when the event originally occurred, like the response of a three-year-old, frozen in time. For instance, I might be aware that my parents divorced when I was three, but when I think about it, it feels like it's happenings right now. The brain treats memory as an ongoing threat, even though it's not. Remember, the amygdala is quick but not clever!

This is what happened to me when I got divorced myself, it triggered childhood memories, and I had such a hard time getting through it, especially without understanding the root cause or where these feelings were coming from. This is also what occurs during flashbacks or intrusive images. When something happens that resembles a traumatic event, the amygdala is activated, responding as though there is a threat. This, in turn, causes us to experience the same emotional response we had at the time of the trauma. The fight-flight-freeze response. These triggers can manifest as various sensations, such as certain smells, body aches, and pains, images, emotions, or even numbness. Experiencing fragmented trauma memories from years ago as an adult, triggered by seemingly harmless events in the present day, can be incredibly confusing. These memories might not be consciously aware to you, yet they exert their influence, impacting your emotional reactions.
Well, that's where trauma work comes in! The idea is to help the brain process the trauma memories, allowing them to be stored in the hippocampus, where they can be filled with time, place, and order. Then, when something triggers the memory, the hippocampus can inform the amygdala, saying "Thanks for warning me, but I know what this is, and there's no threat. Stand

down." the process of making sense of your life involves taking steps that can lead to a much richer, vital, and fulfilling existence, filled with all sorts of fantastic possibilities you may never have dreamed of. If you avoid addressing and making sense of your past, especially if you've experienced extremely difficult events, research shows that you may be more likely to repeat them, whether it's abuse, neglect, emotional distance, or any other challenging experiences. However, we need to recognize that this work can be challenging and people might feel scared. The key is to empower individuals by acknowledging that it's not only about what happened to them but also about how they make sense of what happened. The great news from neuroplasticity is that we have the power to change our lives. We can use the ability to look at the interior world to understand ourselves and others better, ultimately changing the structure and function of the brain for greater integration and awareness. This, in turn, leads to increased flexibility and adaptability, fostering a profound sense of vitality within us, resulting in a more harmonious life. Such possibilities lie ahead.

At times, we might notice the ego sneaking in through the back door during our healing journey, especially when our healing process is driven by the desire to be self-sufficient. The archetypes of ultra-independence, the lone wolf, and the hyper-individualistic approach to healing all share a common thread— they cater to the ego's desires.

There is a great risk involved in opening ourselves to connection and vulnerability with others. Sometimes, what may seem like healing is merely sealing the entryways that lead to the heart. The path of relationships is one of the most challenging because we relinquish control and often confront the most wounded and fearful parts of ourselves, which can easily dismiss or overlook when we're alone.

The idea that true healing means we no longer need anyone is misleading; it is in fact, a trauma response. It represents the ego acting as a gatekeeper, shielding the heart from the possibility of getting hurt again. But if not for connection and genuine belonging, then what is the purpose of it all?

To truly accept our primal needs for community and connection, we must confront ourselves in the shadows, acknowledging the pride that defends us from being truly seen.

We are not here to be lone wolves, disconnected from others and the world around us. The belief that we should all be entirely self-sufficient has led us to a point in time with significant imbalances of power, equality, and access to food and resources. We are not here to learn how to become needless; that desire to remain separate stems from our wounds. Don't let the ego win. Even in moments when you feel like closing your heart and giving up, remember that your pain doesn't isolate you from others. You are not alone in your suffering, and your story doesn't have to end here. Instead, let your past experiences serve as a reminder of your resilience rather than evidence of an unsafe world.

Life isn't trying to break you down; it's trying to break you open.

Chapter 2: Destiny and relationships

All human beings share the same deepest longings: to know and be known, to hold and be held, to love and be loved, to experience connection without walls and expression without censorships. And yet, when real love presents itself when a loving partner stands before you, you may notice a disconcerting urge to withdraw, put up walls, or even run. Love can be intimidating.

Why are so many people scared of love?

Many people fear relationships because they have a fear of love. Deep within this urge lies the subconscious awareness that love means opening oneself to the possibility of getting hurt through loss or rejection by the one you love. By holding back from the relationship, they limit the intimacy and, in turn, protect themselves against the potential risk.

We have numerous defenses to protect ourselves from the risk of loss. Some of these defenses are obvious and well known: We use sarcasm or dry humor to downplay moments of vulnerability, create distractions like work and busyness, or constantly check our smartphones, becoming addicted to screens. Often without realizing it, these actions stem from the fear of love.

Other defense mechanisms that hinder intimacy are more subtle. They occur in the realm of the mind and usually manifest as doubt. While healthy doubt has its place, especially when addressing red flags in a relationship, doubt in a healthy relationship can be a very sneaky defense mechanism rooted in the fear of loss.

Yet, destiny plays a tremendous role in our lives. No one can change their destiny. What is destined will happen!

Good or bad, you have to go through it. However, the choice is yours. You can either accept things happily or sadly. Destiny is not entirely within a person's control, as some of your friends might have claimed. Hard work is the only aspect you can control, yet even after putting in lots of hard work, success may not be guaranteed!

What do you call it then? You work harder and still achieve the same results. This suggests that there might be someone up there who has full control over our lives, which we call destiny.

Take life as it comes! God sees a person through both bad times and good times, teaching us tolerance and patience. Destiny, no matter how hard we try, remains unchanged. Life is filled with ups and downs, and these events seem predestined. While our choices can shape our future to some extent, destiny still holds the upper hand in shaping us differently. But if there is destiny, where does free will come in? The fact is that God has provided us with the infrastructure of life, including support systems and various situations that come our way, this is the destiny part. However, our responses to these situations, guided by our core understanding, knowledge, and information, represent our free will or freedom of choice. In this aspect, we are entirely free. Thus it becomes a 50-50 matter. Destiny plays a 50 percent role that we cannot change, and the other 50 percent plays our free will. We have complete freedom to respond to situations as we see fit. Theodore Roosevelt once said: "Believe you can, and you're halfway there." To me, this means that accomplishing anything requires more than just overcoming external forces like destiny and working hard; it also involves conquering the power of our minds. If we don't believe in ourselves, who will?

It still holds that meaning, but what about the times when halfway is the furthest you can go? Is halfway sometimes okay? I don't mean a scenario where you believe you can do something but never attempt it. I am referring to having a goal, believing or knowing you can achieve it, working hard towards that goal, and then realizing at some point that it's not going to work out. At this juncture, you are faced with a crossroads: to stop or to continue. In such cases, I believe destiny is testing you to see if you truly want to pursue this path or if you have changed your mind.

This freedom of choice has opened doors for two kinds of people: those who lead toward success and those who head toward failure. All our successes, failures, and actions are influenced by the decisions we make in the present moment. If we make correct decisions and act accordingly, no one can prevent us from achieving our goals. If we encounter failure, it's an opportunity for learning and growth, a chance to start again with new insights.

We have the option to make decisions using our free will and take full responsibility for our actions. In this line of thinking, many consider fate a superstition at worst and, at best, view it as a psychological defense system to cope with life's failures. Whenever we fail in an endeavor or face something that doesn't align with our wishes, it's tempting to use fate as a convenient scapegoat. We might attribute it to bad luck or other people's interventions that caused us to fail. However, in reality, many of us struggle to accept that we are responsible for our own failures. It could be due to poor planning, lack of effort in the right direction, making the wrong choice of a partner, or outright failure to accurately assess the realities of our goal.

Success or failure can also depend on how you react in certain circumstances. Our reaction to situations can lead us to either success or failure. When we react in a way that creates conflict with others, it becomes an opportunity to assess how we handle cooperation in difficult situations. Conflict is a normal part of any healthy relationship, as two people can't be expected to agree on everything, all the time. The key is not to fear or try to avoid conflict but to learn how to resolve it healthily. When conflict is mismanaged, it can cause significant harm to a relationship. However, when handled respectfully and positively, conflict provides an opportunity to strengthen the bond between two people. This principle applies to every aspect of your life.

Conflict usually arises from differences of opinion, occurring whenever people disagree over their values, motivations, perceptions, ideas, or desires. Sometimes these differences may seem trivial, but when a conflict triggers strong emotions, a deep personal need is often at the core of the problem. These needs can range from the need to feel safe and secure or respected and valued, to the need to be heard and understood, and even the need for greater closeness and intimacy. Consider the opposing needs of a toddler and a parent. The child's need is to explore, so venturing to the street or the cliff edge fulfills that need. However, the parent's need is to protect the child's safety, which can only be met by limiting the toddler's exploration. Since these needs conflict, it gives rise to a disagreement. The needs of each party play an important role in the long-term success of relationships with others, and each deserves respect and consideration. In personal relationships, a lack of understanding about differing needs can result in distance, arguments, and break-ups. In the workplace, differing needs can result in broken deals, decreased profits, and lost jobs. When you can recognize conflicting needs and are willing to examine them with compassion and understanding, it can lead to creative problem-solving, team building, and stronger relationships.

Relationships are one of the most important aspects of our lives, yet we often overlook just how crucial our connections with other people are for our physical and mental health and well-being. Those who are more socially connected to family, friends, or their community tend to be happier, physically healthier and live longer, experiencing fewer mental health problems compared to those who are less well-connected.

It's not merely about the number of friends you have, nor is it solely based on being in a committed relationship; the quality of your close relationships is what truly matters. Living in conflict or within a toxic relationship can be more damaging than being alone.

As a society and as individuals, we must urgently prioritize investing in building and maintaining good relationships and addressing the barriers that hinder forming them. Neglecting this aspect is equivalent to turning a blind eye to the impact of smoking and obesity on your health and well-being.

The Mental Health Foundation defines relationships as how two or more people are connected or the state of being connected. Relationships include the intimate bonds we have with our respective partners, those we form with our parents, siblings, and grandparents, as well as the social connections we establish with friends, work colleagues, teachers, healthcare professionals, and the community.

Extensive evidence shows that having good-quality relationships can help us to live longer, happier lives with fewer mental health problems. Having close, positive relationships can give us a sense of purpose and belonging.

Loneliness and isolation remain key predictors of poor psychological and physical health. Poor self-esteem, characterized by a lack of self-worth, often arises when significant people in your life are critical towards you, or when you are a perfectionist and overly critical of yourself. In either case, the tendency is to harshly judge, ignore, or downplay the importance of real accomplishments, even when it makes no sense to act this way.

There may also be a belief present that self-worth can only be based on the acclaim of other popular high-status individuals, even though this is not the case. Studies have shown that a lack of good relationships and long-term feelings of loneliness are associated with higher rates of mortality, poor physical health outcomes, lower life satisfaction, and loss of self.

Self-efficacy describes how effective and in control people believe they can be in their lives. It is essential for individuals to feel that they have a certain amount of control over their lives to handle difficult situations and meet expected challenges. When people believe they are helpless in altering negative situations, they often find themselves becoming depressed. I know this feeling all too well.

While there are certainly many aspects of life that people cannot control, there is a remarkable number of things that can be influenced. People with low self-efficacy expectations tend to believe they are helpless in influencing their fate and, as a result, may not seek to make positive changes in their lives, even when they are suffering. Self-efficacy tends to be domain-specific; you might feel confident in one area of your life but feel helpless to influence another.

Bullying prevention requires people to have a high level of self-esteem. However, it's essential to note that outside influences can significantly affect your level of self-identity. These external influences include other people, the media, and the content you listen to, read, and watch.

The outside influences you allow into your life can either build up your self-identity or tear it down. You need to pay attention to the messages you receive from other people and the media. Strive to limit negative influences in your life as much as possible if you want to make a positive change in your own life.

The people with whom you surround yourself have a significant effect on your self-identity. The good news is that you get to decide with whom you spend the most time. You have the power to choose whether you spend your time with people who build you up or who tear you down. Even if you develop good habits, like being kinder toward others and taking care of yourself, it will be hard to maintain your self-esteem if you consistently hang around people who don't encourage you. If the most important people in your life bring you down, building a healthy level of self-esteem will be very difficult. It is important to recognize that you have a responsibility to protect your self-identity and your self-esteem. When you encounter people who seek to drag you down, choose to spend less time with them. Additionally, avoid those who are nervous perfectionists, unkind, or discourage you from reaching your goals. Instead, invest your time in forming positive relationships with those who build you up and encourage you to grow. Surrounding yourself with positive people will not only help you to become a better person but also allow you to maintain or increase your level of self-worth.

Another crucial aspect to consider in forming your self-identity is understanding that nothing good comes from comparing yourself to others, especially if it becomes a habit. Comparing yourself to others is a destructive pattern that tears down your self-esteem. Why? Because when you compare yourself to others, you can never truly win. Think about it: there will always be someone better than you, who has more, or who has accomplished more than you have. When you constantly measure yourself against others and their achievements, you rob yourself of the ability to appreciate who you are and all that you already have. We are all unique individuals with different skill sets, life experiences, opportunities, and backgrounds. Instead of comparing yourself to others, try comparing your present self to your potential for improvement. This will provide the encouragement you need to keep growing and help you stay motivated to elevate yourself in the process.

In addition to the people in your life, pay attention to what you read, listen to, and watch. Many TV channels or magazines only seek to glorify celebrities while telling the readers or viewers that they should be losing weight, making more money, buying certain products, etc. This kind of media influence can make people feel bad about themselves or as though they are not good enough. Such influences can damage self-esteem and tear people down. Spending more time on the internet, reading magazines, or watching gossip-filled TV shows can leave you feeling unsure about yourself in the long run. Instead, use that time to build yourself up. Seek a balance and engage with media sources like books, blogs, websites, or podcasts that affirm you, help you grow, and make you feel good about yourself. However, have you ever experienced a lack of motivation or felt unsure of why you don't want to do anything?? One of the most frustrating things in life is losing the drive to be productive. It can be disheartening to know that you have wonderful people and things going on in your life, yet you can't seem to enjoy them fully. In many cases, we may not be aware that feeling lazy may be a sign that we need to attend to our mental health, and wellness, and engage in self-care.

Feeling unmotivated or apathetic towards life can happen to the best of us from time to time, and it can especially affect young adults. Abuse survivors and sexual assault victims often report high levels of apathy. Something is preventing you from feeling motivated, but you just don't know what it is. This is especially true if these feelings have been persisting for a long time. It may seem as if these feelings have appeared out of nowhere, and suddenly, you find yourself lacking the motivation to do anything. You might start saying things like, "I feel fine, so why can't I find the motivation to do anything? What's wrong with me?"

Your family may observe you going about your day lackluster and attribute it to laziness, but unless you are knowingly choosing not to do anything, there may be more to it. Many people suffering from depression experience a loss of interest or energy. It may feel as if all of these feelings are completely out of your control, and you may need some assistance to regain control if necessary. If all you feel like doing is lying on the couch and watching TV rather than going outside and engaging with life, especially if this feeling persists, there may be an underlying mental health condition affecting you negatively. These feelings can be situational, such as after experiencing a break-up or while being sick. Alternatively, they can be more long-term in the form of depression, where feelings of hopelessness and sadness linger. In such situations, it is important not to give up but instead identify the source of these emotions and seek solutions to cope with them. On the other hand, some of us may simply be introverts, which is a personality trait.

What about long-term relationships that lead to marriages? It's interesting how many individuals react with a somewhat sad face when asked about having too much fun being single. Today, someone told me in a chat, 'Being single is so much fun! I wonder how long the fun will last, though, especially while all my friends are getting married and having kids."

I responded, saying, "You should never get married to someone for the wrong reasons. And those reasons include:
- Pressure from friends and family.

- Feeling lonely because they were single and settling for the first person that comes along.
- Everyone around your circle is married or having kids.
- Being together for images, as the relationship looks good on paper (or in photos), but the two people involved don't admire each other.
- Being young, naive, and hopelessly in love, thinking that love will solve everything.
- Entering a relationship to try to fix yourself.

This desire to use someone else's love to soothe your emotional problems inevitability leads to codependence, creating an unhealthy and damaging dynamic between two people where they tacitly agree to use each other's love as a distraction from their own self-loathing. We will delve more into codependence later, but for now, it's essential to point out that love itself is neutral. It can be both healthy or unhealthy, helpful or harmful, depending on the reasons and ways you love someone and are loved by them. Love, by itself, is never enough to sustain a relationship.

I believe that the right reasons that make a relationship "work" (by work, I mean that it is happy and sustainable for both people involved) require a genuine, deep-level admiration for each other. Without that mutual admiration, everything else will unravel.

Before entering a relationship, you must have realistic expectations about relationships and romance.
- Communication and respect are among the most important aspects of building a loving and lasting relationship.
- Talk openly about everything, especially the things that hurt, and be open to discussing and working through them.
- Give each other space.
- A healthy relationship means two healthy individuals.
- Learn to handle conflicts effectively and practice forgiveness.

- Remember, the little things add to the big things. Sex matters a lot, and it's worth investing in.

The relationship is a living, breathing thing. Much like the body and muscles, it cannot get stronger without stress and challenges. You have to fight. You have to hash things out. Overcoming obstacles makes the marriage stronger.

John Gottman is a well-respected psychologist and researcher who has spent over 30 years analyzing married couples, seeking keys to understanding why they stay together or break up. Chances are, if you've read any relationship advice before, you've either directly or indirectly been exposed to his work. When it comes to answering the question, "Why do people stay together?" he dominates the field.

What Gottman does is he gets married couples in a room, puts some cameras on them, and then he asks them to fight.

Notice: he doesn't ask them to talk about how great the other person is. He doesn't ask them what they like best about their relationship. He asks them to fight. He wants them to pick something they're having problems with and discuss it for the camera.

By simply analyzing the film for the couple's discussion (or shouting match, whatever it may be), he's able to predict with startling accuracy whether a couple will divorce or not. But what's most interesting about Gottman's research is that the things that lead to divorce are not necessarily what you think. Successful couples, like unsuccessful couples, he found, fight consistently. And some of them fight furiously.

He has been able to narrow down four characteristics of a couple that tend to lead to divorces (or breakups). He has gone on to call these "the four horsemen" of the relationship apocalypse in his books. They are:

1. Criticizing your partner's character ("You're so stupid" vs. "That thing you did was stupid")
2. Defensiveness (or, blame-shifting, "I wouldn't have done that if you weren't late all the time")
3. Contempt (putting down your partner and making them feel inferior)
4. Stonewalling (withdrawing from an argument and ignoring your partner)

Conclusion:

Never insult or name-call your partner. Put another way: hate the sin, love the sinner. Gottman's research found that "contempt" — belittling and demeaning your partner — is the number one predictor of divorce.

Do not bring previous fights/arguments into current ones. This solves nothing and only makes the current fight twice as bad as it was before. Yes, you forgot to pick up groceries on the way home, but what does his being rude to your mother last Thanksgiving have to do with anything?

If things get too heated, take a breather. Remove yourself from the situation and come back once your emotions have cooled off a bit. This is a big one for me sometimes when things get intense, I get overwhelmed and just leave for a while. Then I come back, and we're both a bit calmer, and we can resume the discussion with a much more conciliatory tone.

Remember that being right is not as important as both people feeling respected and heard. You may be right, but if you express it in a way that makes your partner feel unloved, then there's no real winner.

I think when people talk about the necessity for "good communication" all the time, it means being willing to have uncomfortable conversations. Speak the ugly truth and get it all out in the open, and be willing to clarify and find solutions together.

You and your partner will grow and change in unexpected ways: embrace it.

Relationships can shape the self-concept, bring out unique aspects of our personality, and influence our perspectives and goals. Yet, the self is not a passive player in relationships, as self-related goals and motives can also influence how relationships form and develop. That's why learning how to have a successful relationship is important for our well-being and shapes our identity in the best way possible.

You can work through anything as long as you are not destroying yourself or each other. That means emotionally, physically, financially, or spiritually. Make nothing off-limits to discuss. Never shame or mock each other for the things that make you happy. Prioritize each other.

Chapter 3: Personality traits

What is personality? How do you develop your unique self? The word personality itself stems from the Latin word persona, which refers to a theatrical mask worn by performers to either project different roles or disguise their identities.

At its most basic, personality is the characteristic patterns of thoughts, feelings, and behaviors that make a person unique. It is believed that personality arises from within the individual and remains fairly consistent throughout life. While there are many different definitions of personality, most focus on the pattern of behaviors and characteristics that can help predict and explain a person's behavior.

Explanations for personality can focus on a variety of influences, ranging from genetic explanations for personality traits to the role of the environment and experiences in shaping an individual's personality. So what exactly makes up a personality? Traits and patterns of thought and emotion play important roles, as well as the following fundamental characteristics of personality. One of them is consistency, which is generally recognizable in the order and regularity of behaviors.

Essentially, people tend to act in similar ways or exhibit consistent behaviors in a variety of situations. Personality is influenced not only by psychological and physiological factors but also by biological processes and needs. It only shapes how we move and respond in our environment but also influences our thoughts, feelings, close relationships, and other social interactions.

There are several theories about how personality develops, and different schools of thought in psychology influence many of these theories. Some of the major perspectives on personality include the early type theories. These theories suggest that there is a limited number of "personality types" that are related to biological influences, including:

Type A: perfectionist, impatient, competitive, work-obsessed, achievement-oriented, aggressive, stressed.

Type B: low stress, even-tempered, flexible, creative, adaptable to change, patient, tendency to procrastinate.

Type C: highly conscientious, perfectionist, struggle to reveal emotions (positive and negative).

Type D: feelings of worry, sadness, irritability, pessimistic outlook, negative self-talk, avoidance of social situations, lack of self-confidence, fear of rejection, appearing gloomy, and hopelessness.

Trait theories tend to view personality as the result of internal characteristics that are genetically based and include the following:

Agreeable: cares about others, feels empathy, enjoys helping others.

Conscientiousness: high levels of thoughtfulness, good impulse control, and goal-directed behaviors.

Eager-to-please: accommodating, passive, and conforming.

Extraversion: excitability, sociability, talkativeness, assertiveness, and high amounts of emotional expressiveness.

Introversion: quiet, reserved.

Neuroticism: experiences stress and dramatic shifts in mood, feels anxious, worries about different things, gets upset easily, and struggles to bounce back after stressful events.

Openness: very creative, open to trying new things, focuses on tackling new challenges.

Psychodynamic theories of personality are heavily influenced by the work of Sigmund Freud and emphasize the influence of the unconscious mind on personality. Behavioral theories suggest that personality is the result of interactions between the individual and the environment.

Humanist theories emphasize the importance of free will and individual experience in developing a personality. Humanist theorists include Carl Rogers and Abraham Maslow. Research on personality can yield fascinating insights into how personality develops and changes throughout a lifetime. This research can also have important practical applications in the real world. For example, personality assessments are often used to help people learn more about themselves and their unique strengths, weaknesses, and preferences. Some assessments might look at how people rank on specific traits, such as whether they are high in extroversion, conscientiousness, or openness. Other assessments might measure how specific aspects of personality change throughout development. Such personality assessments can also be used to help people determine what careers they might enjoy, how well they might perform in certain job roles, or the effectiveness of a particular form of psychotherapy.

Personality type can also have a connection to your health, including how often you visit the doctor and how you cope with stress. Researchers have found that certain personality characteristics may be linked to illness and health behaviors.

Understanding the psychology of personality is much more than simply an academic exercise. The findings from personality research can have important applications in the world of medicine, health, business, economics, and technology, among others. By building a better understanding of how personality works, we can look for new ways to improve both personal and public health.

So, what personality traits make someone who they are? Each person has an idea of their personality type, whether they are bubbly or reserved, sensitive or thick-skinned.

Psychologists tried to tease out the science of how we define personality as individual differences in the way people tend to think, feel and behave.

How do we measure personality traits? You'll find many quizzes and tests online that claim to measure what personality type. However, most of these are supported by very little evidence, and if you come across a system that claims to break all of humanity into just a handful of categories, it's safe to say it's probably oversimplified. Instead of trying to fit people into rigid "types," each trait occurs along a spectrum, and traits are independent of one another, creating an infinite constellation of human personality.

The traits with the strongest research backing them are the Big Five, some of which were mentioned earlier in this chapter.
1. Openness
2. Conscientiousness
3. Extraversion
4. Agreeableness
5. Neuroticism

Conveniently, you can remember these traits with the handy acronym "The Big Five." They were developed in the 1970s by two research teams. These teams were led by Paul Costa and Robert R. McCrae of the National Institutes of Health, and Warren Norman and Lewis Goldberg of the University of Michigan, according to Scientific American.

How universal are the Big Five? The evidence suggested that these traits translate well across cultures. This suggests that the Big Five personality traits could be a byproduct of living in a large, complex society, while people in small, traditional societies differ along other sets of traits. One possibility is that societies that offer more social niches for people allow more types of personality traits to arise.

If you live in a large, industrialized society, chances are the Big Five will do a pretty good job of summing you up. You might have a dash of openness, a lot of conscientiousness, an average amount of extraversion, plenty of agreeableness, and almost no neuroticism at all. Alternatively, you might be highly conscientious, a bit introverted, disagreeable, neurotic, and barely open. Here's what each trait entails, according to Stephanie Pappas in one of her interesting blogs that I found.

Openness is shorthand for "openness to experience." People who are high in openness enjoy adventure. They're curious and appreciate art, imagination, and new things. The motto of the open individual might be, "Variety is the spice of life."
People low in openness are just the opposite: they prefer to stick to their habits, avoid new experiences, and probably aren't the most adventurous eaters.

Openness might correlate with verbal intelligence and knowledge acquisition over the lifespan. People high in openness enjoy novelty and have a predicted humor production ability above and beyond intelligence.

In other words, they tend to be funnier than people who are just smart.

People who are conscientious are organized and have a strong sense of duty. They're dependable, disciplined, and achievement-focused. You won't find conscientious types getting off on round-the-world journeys without an itinerary; they're planners.

People low in conscientiousness are more spontaneous and freewheeling. At the extreme, they may tend toward carelessness. Conscientiousness is a helpful trait to have, as it has been linked to achievement in school and on the job.

Extraversion versus introversion is possibly the most recognizable personality trait that everyone knows. The more extroverted someone is, the more of a social butterfly they are. Extroverts are chatty, sociable and draw energy from crowds. They tend to be assertive and cheerful in their social interactions.

Introverts, on the other hand, need plenty of alone time. Introversion is often confused with shyness, but the two aren't the same. Shyness implies a fear of social interactions or an inability to function socially. Introverts can be perfectly charming at parties; they just prefer solo or small-group activities. There is another group that has been discovered recently: ambiverts, who have characteristics of both introverts and extroverts. I could put myself in this category.

Agreeableness measures the extent of a person's warmth and kindness. The more agreeable someone is, the more likely they are to be trusting, helpful, and compassionate. Disagreeable people are cold and suspicious of others, and they're less likely to cooperate.

As you might imagine, agreeableness has its benefits. In a study published in Developmental Psychology, agreeable kids had fewer behavioral problems than kids low in agreeableness, and agreeable adults had less depression and greater job stability than adults who were low in agreeableness. However, being agreeable isn't always rewarded. More agreeable people, who tend to be friendly and helpful to others, have significantly lower earnings than less agreeable individuals. It would be nice to keep a balance in knowing when to say "no" and when to say "yes."

I think it's so much easier to say "yes" than it is to say "no" but oftentimes we overwhelm ourselves by saying "yes" when we really want to say "no."

This is, in large part, because we are hard-wired to please people. It can be uncomfortable to tell someone "no" because we don't like how it feels to disappoint someone. Some of us are also afraid of conflict and, to avoid it, will be more agreeable than we want to be. In today's fast-paced, high-tech world, burnout has become common among many of us. That's why your well-being needs to know when to say "yes" and how to say "no".

So, when to say yes? The basic answer to the question is when it feels right to you. Deep inside, we know what we want to do, but when a question arises that we feel compelled to say "no" to, chances are a quick introspection might reveal the reason you're saying no is actually out of fear.

Saying yes to opportunities for advancement, learning, growth, and excitement can lead to countless new experiences that will enrich your life. Say yes to yourself. The word "yes," however, isn't just for others. It's important for us to also say "yes" to ourselves, to permit ourselves to just go for it!

This can be difficult if you are surrounded by naysayers, but trust me, even though friends, family, and colleagues might mean well, at the end of the day, it's your life. Although having moral support is a powerful tool, sometimes you have to trust yourself enough to do what you want to do. For example, when I was in a similar situation and I knew I needed to make some changes to bring balance to my life, I had to tell myself "yes."

Take a breather. While saying yes can lead to adventure and growth, be sure that you're not spreading yourself too thin by agreeing too often. Before you say yes to someone, take a deep breath. Give yourself that little extra time to focus on what you truly want before you agree to it. Breathing is a powerful way to regroup and center yourself.

Then, how to say no? Strangely, one of the smallest words is also one of the most difficult for many of us to say. But knowing different ways to say no can help alleviate our fear of conflict and propel us towards a more fulfilling life.

One of the ways I was using it in saying "no" was by giving myself some time to think. For example, when someone asks me to come to an event, I would say "Thank you so much for the invitation; it sounds lovely. Let me see if I will be able to attend," and then I take some time to think, checking my schedule and considering how this event makes me feel. If this makes me feel uncomfortable or that I won't enjoy it, then I politely say no.

You don't need to explain why you are saying no, which is something many people struggle with. The truth is if the person you're saying "no" wants to know why, you can choose to explain it, but the reality is that it's your choice to say no regardless of the reason.

While it's not a good idea to leave people hanging, sometimes it's helpful to tell them you will get back to them or ask them to let you think about it. This gives you time to evaluate the situation and decide if you want to say yes or no. Keep your answer simple. Sometimes simply saying, "Thank you so much for asking me. While it is not something I'd like to do, please know how honored I am that you felt you could ask me."

When I learned to say "no" to people and to events I didn't want. I could see the world through different lenses. Some people cannot take "no" for an answer, and they may react aggressively or competitively. This helped me filter those people out of my life more quickly than when I was more agreeable and a people pleaser. I could see their true personality, their real selves. I was shocked to witness how people respond to a simple "no". Well, I still think that anything that irritates us reveals some unhealed parts within ourselves. Perhaps those who react negatively to a simple "no" experienced childhood traumas where their parents said "no" all the time, and as they grew up, this unhealed wound affected their interactions with other people.

I think many people have heard this quote: "Your perception of me is a reflection of you; my reaction to you is an awareness of me." This quote has popped up many times in my social feeds. Today, more than ever, this quote comes full circle for me. How many times have we been trapped in others' skewed perceptions of us? Perception is merely just that, it's the stories we tell ourselves combined with how we interpret our interactions with others and the associated meanings we attach to those interactions. It's about the person perceiving and the lens through which they see their world. How people treat others is a reflection of how they feel about themselves.

When the person becomes aggressive, I imagine that they may say "no" to themselves so much that it even hurts to hear it. This way, it doesn't affect me. I just feel compassion and distance myself from the person. I move forward toward the things that make me happy and help me achieve my goals.

Which brings me to the neuroticism personality trait. It is a type of personality in which the person places blame on their dysfunctional parents, criticizes others, and has difficulty saying "no." They worry about everything and obsess over minor details. Some individuals even fixate on germs to the extent that I once knew someone who quit a job due to overwhelming anxiety about not having access to a private bathroom.

People with high neuroticism worry frequently and easily slip into anxiety and depression. Although, even when neurotic people with good salaries earned raises, the extra income made them less happy. This is because people high in neuroticism tend to experience a lot of negative emotions. According to a paper published in Clinical Psychological Science, neuroticism plays a role in the development of emotional disorders.

In contrast, people who are low in neuroticism tend to be emotionally stable and even-keeled.

Personality was once thought to be very difficult to alter, but evidence is accumulating that personality can change in adulthood. The real change happens within you, and it can only occur when you deeply desire it.

Chapter 4: The self-healing

To uncover who we are and why we act the way we do, we must delve into our own story. Being brave and willing to explore our past is an important stepping stone on the path to understanding ourselves and becoming who we want to be. Research has shown that it isn't solely the events that shape us, but also the extent to which we have made sense of those experiences. Unresolved traumas from our history influence our present behaviors.

The attitudes and atmosphere in which we grew up heavily influence our behavior as adults. Painful early life experiences often shape and influence our behavior in subtle ways we may not even be aware of. For example, having a harsh parent may lead us to become more guarded, always feeling defensive or resistant to new challenges due to the fear of being ridiculed. Carrying this uncertainty into adulthood can shake our sense of identity and limit us in different areas. To break free from this pattern of behavior, it's valuable to acknowledge its underlying drivers. We must be willing to look at the sources of our most self-limiting or self-destructive tendencies.

When we try to conceal or evade our past experiences, we can feel lost, as if we don't truly know ourselves. Consequently, we may act automatically without understanding why.

In his book *Mindsight: The New Science of Personal Transformation*, "Dr. Siegel recounts an interaction with his son during which he lost his temper. After reflecting on the incident later, Dr. Siegel realized that his emotional outburst had more to do with feelings he had as a child toward his brother than with his perception of his son in the present moment.

He wrote about the experience, "I realize once again how many layers of meaning our brain contains, and how quickly old, perhaps forgotten, memories can emerge to shape our behavior. These associations can make us act on automatic pilot."

Through reflecting on the past, using a technique called mindsight, "which involves focused attention to observe the internal workings of our minds," Dr. Siegel was able to find meaning in his experience and subsequently discuss the incident with his son to mend the situation. He explained, "With hindsight, I could utilize the reflections that emerged from that conflict to gain more clarifying insights into my own childhood experiences. These challenging moments in our lives can be transformed into opportunities to deepen our self-understating and strengthen our connections with others."

Engaging in this type of thinking and embracing the memories that arise allows us to gain invaluable insights into our behavior. Consequently, we can consciously separate ourselves from the more harmful influences from our past and actively alter our behavior to align with our true thoughts, feelings, and choices in the world.

There is a video on the Internet that I often watch when I am feeling down, and it is incredibly motivational. They say "Know that you're going to experience ups and downs. Most people give up on themselves too easily. Do you know how powerful the human spirit is? There is nothing quite as powerful. Every time you endure pain and handle it positively, you grow stronger within. You become unbroken, unstoppable. It's hard to crush the human spirit!

Anybody can feel good when they have good health, their bills are paid, and they have happy relationships. It's easy to be positive and have a larger vision under such circumstances. Anyone can have faith then. However, the real challenge of growth, mentally, emotionally, and spiritually, arises when you get knocked down. It takes courage to act, especially when you feel defeated. It takes courage to rise from the fall and start over again. Fear has the power to kill dreams, extinguish hope, and even put people in the hospital. It can age you and hold you back from achieving your true potential. Fear can paralyze you, preventing you from doing what you know deep down you are capable of achieving.

Remember, at the end of your feelings lies nothing, but at the end of every principle lies a promise. Behind your little feelings, there might be nothing significant, but behind every principle stands a promise. If you find yourself not reaching your goals, it may be because you're overly focused on your feelings. Don't let your feelings dictate your actions. Push beyond them, and remember that your true strength lies in the principles you uphold, not in momentary emotions.

Every day you say "no" to your dreams, you might be pushing them back by six months, even a whole year! That single day, the one day you didn't get up, could have set you back for who knows how long. Don't allow your emotions to control you. While it's natural to have emotions, you need to start disciplining them. If you don't, they will use you. If you truly want something, you will have to work for it. It won't be easy; change rarely is. If it were easy, everyone would achieve their dreams. But if you are truly committed, you will go all out and declare, 'I am in control here. I won't let this setback get me down; it won't destroy me. I am coming back, and I will emerge stronger and better because of it.

You've got to make a declaration. Stand up for what you believe in—your dreams, peace of mind, and health. Take full responsibility for your life, accept where you are, and commit to taking yourself where you want to go. Decide to live each day as if it were your last, and embrace life with passion and drive. Push yourself and recognize that the last chapter of your life has not been written yet. The past doesn't define you; what truly matters is what you will do about it."

With this mindset, I am feeling fearless and unstoppable, even in the face of negative situations. Fate loves the fearless. There is nothing more powerful than a humble person with a warrior spirit, driven by a higher purpose.

There is no problem in this world without a solution. Some may be easier to solve, while others might be challenging, but with an open mind and a positive outlook, you can find the best approach to any negative situation. You will overcome it. You can heal your wounds and find your true self. It's tough, but we must also realize that without any pain, life has no meaning. Just like when you work out at the gym, you initially feel the pain in your muscles, and muscle growth can be painful. Even a paper cut can hurt unexpectedly. When we learn to be resilient, we embrace the diverse spectrum of the human experience.

Once you develop resilience after experiencing the first painful event, it will be there for you the next time you face adversity. Resilience is like a muscle that needs to be exercised and strengthened. If you have already developed it, it can grow when you face adversity again. Remember that all of us will face difficult times in our lives. The important questions to ask yourself are: Can you get through it? Can you grow through it? Can you learn from it? When we view adversities as opportunities for growth and learning, they become valuable experiences. As Ernest Hemingway once wrote, "Everyone is broken by life, but afterward, some people are stronger in broken places."

Before we are born, our Higher Self meticulously configures the environment, family, circumstances, and scenarios that will best serve our evolutionary journey. Lisa Bourbeau in her book "Heal your wounds and find your true self" said that we grow when we accept responsibility for our actions, beliefs, and attitudes, and the process of self-healing is the path to expanding our conscious awareness. Through healing, we become more active, confident, and happy. Shadow work involves confronting the ego and our inner child. It can be messy, difficult, and emotional as we journey inward, but it is from this introspection that we find release, bliss, freedom, and ultimately light. Bourbeau outlines five masks that correspond to fundamental human wounds, which we use to protect ourselves from further pain and suffering. We all experience triggers, and we carry these emotional cards within our physical bodies.

When we realize there is a mind-body-soul connection, we can systematically identify the source of our pain and heal it. Life is a metaphysical healer, and this is a practical and profound way we should all focus on if we want to be truly happy. We create our happiness; everything we want in life can be found within ourselves. Books can teach us a lot, but true wisdom comes from sitting alone in silence with our soul and hearing it speak. The answers we seek are within.

We need to pay more attention to our mental health, and our psychological, emotional, and social well-being, as they impact every area of our lives. Having positive mental health allows us to effectively deal with the daily stressors of life, communicate well with others, make healthy decisions, and live life to its fullest. Life becomes even more beautiful when you open your eyes to see it. Nature possesses a remarkable ability to heal itself and offers valuable lessons on how to heal ourselves.

That brings me back to history. After reading and evaluating the works and writing of some of the most influential philosophers of the Romantic era, I can only conclude that "we are only human." According to the concept of the healing power of nature, romantics sought to reclaim human freedom by respecting nature and finding peace with it. They were introspective, and the concept of romantic love was prominent in every artist's music, paintings, and writings. Although the healing power of nature may seem to be a long-lost remedy from the Native Americans, Henry David Thoreau and William Wordsworth see it not as a form of medicine, but rather as a state of mind. After cultivating a sensible state of mind, one can only assume that their heart will follow suit, enchanting ideas of romantic love, which are evident in the works of Heinrich Heine, John Keats, and William Wordsworth. All of these great philosophers and writers lived in a period called the Romantic Era. The word "romantic" actually has no real fixed meaning, and other romantics would argue for its different interpretations. This era was characterized by creativity and the free expression of emotions, rejecting the imperialistic ideas from the previous Enlightenment era. Let us first discover the Healing Power of Nature as described by William Wordsworth, Henry David Thoreau, and Jean-Jaques Rousseau.

The Healing Power of Nature in this era was not considered medicine or a remedy for any illness one might have. It was the understanding of Mother Nature, the understanding that nature was to be respected as a force rather than neglected and exploited for human waste. We need to return to our basics and rediscover that humans are creatures endowed with reason. As creatures, we should not be living our lives driven solely by economic necessity, but rather by understanding our inner selves and aligning with nature. Let nature heal your worries and mend your troubled mind. In Henry David Thoreau's book, *Walden*, he retreats to the woods to live for two years so that he could live deliberately and renew himself. He goes on to describe the place where he built his cabin, a place free from the noisy tales of gossip and so-called news. When talking about the news, he says "If you have learned the history of her crops for an average year, you never need to attend to that thing again unless your speculations are merely pecuniary character…Shams and delusions are esteemed as the soundest truths, while reality is considered fictitious. If we would consistently observe realities only and not allow ourselves to be deluded, life when compared to such things we know, would be like fairy tales. If we respected only what is inevitable and had the right to be, music, and poetry would resound along the streets. When we are unhurried and wise, we perceive that only great and worthy things have any permanent and absolute existence and that petty fears and pleasures are but shadows of reality."

After going through a divorce, I returned to my childhood home to recharge and heal. During a camping trip with friends, I had the opportunity to witness nature in its purest form, much like Thoreau describes in his writings. His words allowed me to perceive nature in new ways, free from the distractions of ringing cell phones, blaring traffic music, and the hectic rush of city life. This experience made me truly appreciate the gifts of nature and the fortunate upbringing I had. Nature is an essential part of our existence; without it, we are nothing. It embodies reality, freeing us from the worries of schedules and appearances. At that moment, I understood the deeper meaning behind Thoreau's words, "If we respected only what is inevitable and has a right to be." Humans come and go in the blink of an eye on this Earth, but nature continues to rejuvenate itself repeatedly, representing the ultimate truth and reality. As human beings, we must allow nature to revive and rejuvenate us as well.

In the past few hundred years, there has been an increasing distance between humans and the natural environment. Studies exploring the relationship between humans and natural settings have provided evidence of the health benefits of being in contact with nature. While we may not be able to reside in grasslands or forests, we should make an effort to spend more time in parks or flower gardens. Nature plays an important role in human health, and parks or other natural settings offer people the opportunity to get connect with nature. It is safe to say that a "collaboration' between health promotion agencies and nature would be a wise choice for human health, as it has helped me tremendously. Every individual and community should take advantage of the natural gifts from nature in terms of human health. Moreover, we should all create more opportunities to experience the benefits of being in contact with nature from time to time, addressing existing and emerging health problems.

I firmly believe that spending time outdoors is inherently healing. The sensory impact of being in nature has both general and specific positive effects on our health. In today's culture, where we often spend excessive amounts of time indoors and on our technology devices, we are missing a key ingredient for maintaining good health. The healing power of nature recognizes the body's natural ability to heal itself, starting at the cellular level. Cells the fundamental blocks of the body, are dynamic and living entities constantly working towards self-repair and regeneration. For example, when you get a cut or scrape, your body springs into action. Blood platelets gather and clot to protect the wound, while blood vessels deliver fresh nutrients and oxygen to facilitate healing. White blood cells gather at the site to protect against infection, and red blood cells arrive to construct new tissue. It's a remarkable process that halts when healing is complete. Isn't it fascinating to witness our body's remarkable capability for self-healing?

The interesting fact I learned is that self-healing extends beyond the skin level. The body diligently supports recovery from injuries and illnesses on its own. Daily and automatically, damaged, destroyed, or dead cells are replaced in your major organ systems. When you contract a virus, your immune system launches an attack. The digestive system consistently replaces old cells lining the gastrointestinal tract with newer ones. Even when you break a bone, bone cells kick into action to facilitate the healing and growth process.

However, certain genetic, environmental, and behavioral/lifestyle factors may slow or prevent optimal healing and recovery. These individually unique factors can interfere with the body's inherent ability to heal. Similarly, our mental health can be affected. When you're trying to deal with depression, turning your attention inward can be beneficial. Even if you're already undergoing treatment with medication and therapy, tending to your inner self can lift your spirit and enhance your emotional management.

Incorporating various activities, such as meditation or simply having fun, can be part of the healing plan. However, it's essential to start with small steps. Choose one thing that resonates with you and make it a habit. With time, these small changes will accumulate into more significant improvements.

At some point, you will make a decision. You will choose to embrace where you are rooted and decide to be happy right where you stand because happiness is within your control. The contentment we seek can be discovered within ourselves. While you hold onto dreams, you also allow yourself to create new ones and expand your aspirations. Instead of waiting for perfection, you craft a life that feels beautiful, wonderful, and full of possibilities exactly where you are. Take a moment to look around and feel gratitude for what you have already accomplished. Embrace simple joys and easy pleasures, and take up a hobby that brings you joy.

Instead of constantly forcing things, let go of unnecessary control. Look at the raw materials of your life and realize that "I can make something extraordinary with this." Start building, right from where you're planted. Don't wait for everything to align perfectly; rather, align it yourself, brick by brick. A beautiful life does not simply happen; you can create it. By understanding who you are, you also discover what you can create and achieve in certain situations. You have the power to choose how you react. It all comes down to you.

Healing takes time; it is a process, a journey of discovery. One day, with the benefit of retrospect, everything will make sense to you. This life journey is the reason you had to endure all that pain and feel stuck for years. It's why you needed to delve deep into yourself, cultivate self-belief, and prepare for something greater. Letting go of things that no longer serve you allows you to learn self-love and find your true self. Healing before everything falls into place is essential. You may wonder why it hurts and why sadness overwhelms you, but one day, all these experiences will align and make sense. Every aspect of your life weaves together to form a unique tapestry. Trust that, even in the darkest and uncertain times, you are being guided somewhere meaningful. Have faith that a higher force is leading you toward magic, synchronicities, and the eventual convergence of all aspects of your life. One day, you will look back and say, 'Ah, that's why.' Trust in the process, for it is shaping and preparing you for what lies ahead. If you feel lost, it means you're venturing into new territory. Being lost can be a beautiful place to discover yourself. As humans, especially in today's society, we often unconsciously adhere to a predefined timeline, not allowing ourselves the grace or permission to deviate from its expectations. However, feeling lost can also mean that you're free – free to explore new ideas, destinations, and habits, and meet new people. It can be the beginning of self-discovery if you choose to see it that way.

In life, not everything goes as planned. We must work towards our bigger dreams and become examples for future generations and those around us. A.D. Williams once said, "Imagine what 7 billion humans could accomplish if we loved and respected one another." Just imagine that. Picture a world without greed or comparison, where everyone runs their race while cheering for others at the same time.

Start with yourself. Choose to lift others and set an example. Prioritize healing yourself and becoming a role model for kindness and integrity. Demonstrate compassion and understanding in your actions. As the quote goes "No matter how educated, talented, rich, or cool you believe you are, how you treat people ultimately tells all. Integrity is everything." This quote rings true, as who you are is defined by more than your possessions; it's about how you make others feel. Be kind to each other, especially in a world where you can be anything. Choose to embody the change you wish to see in the world. Don't wait for someone else to act first; take the initiative to be an example of kindness. Because you never know how much a person may be suffering inside. Your words, presence, and actions can make a significant difference in someone's life. Be the reason someone else decides to make a difference in the lives of others. Be the influence you want to see more of in the world. Always choose to do what is right, not what is easy at the moment. Kindness is contagious, like a virus. When you do good to others, it inspires them to do better for those they encounter. You have the power to make a significant impact on the world, not just today but every day. Anne Frank once said: "In the long run, the sharpest weapon of all is a kind and gentle spirit."

No one has ever achieved greatness by belittling others. Instead, be kind and always strive to uplift others to the best of your ability. Treat everyone with the same level of kindness that you would like for yourself. Not because karma makes no mistakes, but because it is the right thing to do. Show integrity and a genuine desire to leave this world better than when you arrived. To attract more exciting opportunities, embrace the path that life is leading you on. Be open to letting go of strict plans, but never give up on the vision. Believe in yourself and your abilities, for you were put on this earth to realize your greatest potential, live your purpose, and do so courageously understand that true power lies in a humble person with a warrior spirit driven by a higher purpose. It's all about finding a way to work out for you.

Chapter 5: Happiness is a direction to self-realization

As the old cliché goes, "Money can't buy you love". However, money can attract a lot of people who may claim to love you, especially if they know you possess significant amounts of it. But when it comes to love, what are we truly seeking? The answer is happiness!

In matters of love, money, careers, knowledge, travel, friends, family, or anything else, we all, truthfully, seek happiness. Regardless of age, race, gender, nationality, religion, beliefs, and so forth, our ultimate goal is happiness. However, what brings happiness to one person happy may not necessarily bring the same joy to another person. After all, what good is money, love, fame, status, or any achievement if we are not happy or healthy?

The peculiarity of happiness is not only that it varies from person to person but also that it fluctuates from day to day within ourselves. What brought us happiness as children might not do the same as adults. Similarly, what made us happy yesterday may not have the same effect today. So, what exactly is this ever-elusive happiness we all seek? The answer lies in completeness. Unconsciously, we all feel a certain sense of lack and tend to search outside ourselves for something to make us feel whole. Love happens to be one of those experiences that come closest to making us feel content and complete. However, evidence shows that even individuals with massive amounts of wealth still seek love. Conversely, those who have found love may not necessarily be driven by the pursuit of money. I assert that even those who are deeply in love still feel a sense of incompleteness and must continuously make an effort to feel happiness.

The problem with the way most of us seek happiness is that we often utilize the wrong means. We attempt to satisfy our desires through fickle senses, which can lead to perverted ways of stimulation. Consequently, even alcoholics, drug abusers, gluttons, and sex addicts are merely seeking happiness. On the other hand, some individuals reject these temporary pleasures and strive to lead virtuous lives, viewing Heaven as a just reward in the afterlife, promising everlasting happiness.

Happiness is a state of mind for most of us. It is intangible and no matter how we describe our happiness to others, they won't experience the same emotions or sense of satisfaction that we do. If we were to attempt to materialize happiness, it would be likened to the element of fire. Fire, like happiness, has no true definition or form. It simply consumes one substance and transforms it into another. Fire knows no definite borders or outlines, much like the elusive nature of happiness. While we can perceive both we can't fully grasp or hold onto them. Happiness, as experienced by most of us, is ever-changing, forever fleeting, coming and going.

However, there is a lasting happiness that exists, which can be grasped metaphorically if not literally. It is permanent, and its challenges are pronounced, yet it remains ever-replenishing and new. This happiness resides within each of us, whether or not we are conscious of it, as something we all truly seek. Once captured, this inner happiness becomes the only fulfilling achievement that remains ours forever. This ever-burning, eternal happiness within serves as our connection to the Universal Spirit.

As souls, we recognize ourselves as an inherent part of this Oneness, a connection that has no beginning or end. Unfortunately, we often misdirect our quest for this inner presence toward desires and worldly possessions. Nevertheless, worldly attainments can only provide temporary happiness, while the inner happiness of awareness can be permanently sustained. Until we learn how to enjoy and appreciate this treasure within, we will continue to experience continuous disappointment in life. Many people may pass from cradle to grave without ever discovering this lasting happiness or purpose behind their existence.

This lasting inner happiness was referred to by Jesus as "The kingdom of God within you" while Buddha called it Nirvana.

Mystics and yogis refer to it as Samadhi, some as Gnosis, and Shamans and Medicine men as "Great Spirit." New-age thinkers and quantum physicists attempt to analyze it, and the Law of Attraction enthusiasts try to harness it, but it ultimately arises from an inner awakening, a realization that you are not what you merely appear to be. In truth, your consciousness consists of nothing other than the awareness of self. Many refer to this awareness as the "I AM." Through this non-attached state of being, we become inherently connected to all things, one with everything, while still existing beyond the infinite number of things. "This state of consciousness is known as Self-Realization."

It is not an imagined state of being or a mental construct of the mind. It resides beyond the mind and can only be reached through conscious stillness. However, once you find it, you experience completeness and Eternal Bliss. These awakened beings have no desire to bring anyone down or manipulate their environments because their inner joy is independent of all outer experiences or circumstances. Although the desire to be interdependent is a basic human need. We all want to feel connected to one another. The real magic happens when two givers form a connection. This shared state of consciousness is a miracle for others to witness and is often done to inspire others to seek true contentment. It is the source of all genuine fulfillment.

Self-realization has a few broad definitions. In the Western world, it's generally described as the activation of one's full potential of talents and abilities.

Humanistic psychology also follows a similar train of thought regarding self-realization. Psychologist Abraham Maslow has identified individuals he considered to have reached self-realization, including Albert Einstein, Abraham Lincoln, and Eleonor Roosevelt, to name a few. His famous hierarchy of needs theory states that to achieve self-realization (or, in Maslow terms "self-actualization"), one needs to have certain needs met before reaching this stage.

For example, self-realization cannot be fully achieved when struggling financially and preoccupied with worries about paying rent and providing food for your family, among other concerns. Unfortunately, this is the reality for many people, leaving little opportunity for them to maximize their abilities. That's why it is so important to take time for yourself. Meditation has proven to be a great source for finding creative solutions to life's challenges. I know that starting meditation may not be easy initially, as it requires patience and time to sit with yourself and listen to your inner thoughts. Nevertheless, it is necessary for the mind, heart, spirit, and body. Gradually, I started practicing meditation after hearing about its benefits multiple times from various people. Initially, it was annoying, but I committed to myself to sit in a quiet place and meditate for an hour every morning for one week. On the first day, I thought I might go crazy. I would either fall asleep due to years of not getting enough sleep, or my mind would race from one topic to another as I reviewed every experience from my past, I have planned ways to improve my life and wondered why I was sitting in a meditation mode when I could be doing so many other things with this time. However, on the last day, an unexpected and wonderful thing happened. My mind became quiet and entered a state where I could simply witness everything occurring around me without judgment or attachment. I became aware of sounds, sensations in my body, and a profound sense of inner peace. Though thoughts still arose and passed, they did not come at the same rapid pace or of the same nature. Instead, the thoughts were deeper, resembling insights, deeper understandings, and wisdom. I discovered connections I had never seen before and gained a deeper understanding of my motivations, fears, and desires. Creative solutions to problems I had been facing in my life flooded into my consciousness. I felt relaxed, calm, aware, and clearer than ever before. The pressures to perform, prove myself, explain myself, and meet external standards vanished. Instead, I experienced a profound sense of self and purpose in life. When I focused on my deepest, most heartfelt goals and desires, solutions poured into my mind. Clear thoughts and images of steps I needed to take, the people I should talk to, and ways to overcome any obstacles that emerged. It was truly magical. Through meditation sitting with myself, I learned that all the ideas I needed to complete any task, solve any problem, or achieve any goal resided within me, hidden and waiting for me to be discovered.

In religions, the concept of self-realization is viewed from a different perspective altogether. Connecting with your truest self has a lot to do with transcending your mind and body. This self is often considered as an eternal being not confined to the physical space that your mind and body occupy. Many recognize this part of yourself as the soul.

To bring all these definitions together, self-realization ultimately involves finding the answer to the foundational question, "Who am I?"

To answer this question, I believe that what we are is the result of our thought. Our essence is founded on our thoughts; it is shaped by our thoughts. As Buddha said, if a human is happy, it is because they dwell in happy thoughts; if miserable, it is because they dwell in despondent and debilitating thoughts.

Whether one is fearful or fearless, foolish or wise, troubled or serene, the cause of its state lies within that soul, not without. And now, I seem to hear a chorus of voices exclaim, "But do you really mean to say that outward circumstances do not affect our minds?" I do not say that completely, but I assert this as an infallible truth: circumstances can only affect you to the extent that you allow them to do so.

You are swayed by circumstances because you do not have a right understanding of the nature, use, and power of thought.

While your thoughts, feelings, and physical body always changing, you do not change as easily. How often are you distracted, lost in your thoughts, or overwhelmed by difficult emotions?

Being present is more difficult than ever with today's technology. People are often buried in their smartphones or laptops, while those around them crave their attention. Most people spend so little time living in the present. They're either burdened by past hurts and find it hard to let go, or they are preoccupied with worrying about the future. Statistics show that people spend 46.9 percent of their waking hours thinking about something other than what they're doing, and this mind-wandering typically leads them to unhappiness. In that sense, if you tie your fulfillment solely to external circumstances, you become at the mercy of the constantly changing environment. You will only experience a taste of fulfillment when things go your way, when you win, or when you get what you want. A fulfilled human being, a spiritual person knows how to lose; they find fulfillment even in challenging situations. If you do not attach your sense of fulfillment to external circumstances, you can experience fulfillment regardless of what happens. True freedom lies in the ability to be fulfilled independent of environmental conditions. The only thing you have control over is yourself. You can't control the weather, the political situation, and so on, but you can take charge of your decisions, attitude, and reactions. Embrace your fullest potential and take ownership of yourself.

Here are some amazing benefits of self-realization: I have found for myself:

- The ability to monitor your emotions. Instead of being controlled by your emotions, you can now use your observations about them during the experiences to learn how to effectively handle feelings like fear, anxiety, and stress. This newfound skill also enables you to let go of debilitating emotions and embrace empowering ones instead.
- Improved focus and concentration. Guided by your own inner goals and values, self-realization helps you easily identify distractions and eliminate them. By eliminating meaningless things from your life, you can stay committed to what matters most, allowing you to reach your fullest potential and see real results.

- Increased confidence, self-awareness, and self-esteem: By establishing a profound connection with your truest self and freeing yourself from insecurities, worries, and a low sense of self-worth, you can truly grasp the truth that these factors do not define you.
- Becoming more accepting of yourself and others. This newfound self-realization allows you to be more authentic and express emotions freely and clearly. As a result, you can form deeper relationships and spend more time connecting with people, rather than merely trying to impress them.

When people lack a strong sense of self, they become easily influenced by the expectations of others, leading them to live life according to external dictates. Bronnie Ware's renowned work has revealed a profound truth, one of the top regrets expressed by people on their deathbeds is "I wish I'd had the courage to live a life true to myself, not the life others expected of me."

Various pressures, whether from work, society, or even friends and family, can weigh heavily on a person, compelling them to conform to certain norms. Perhaps a challenging upbringing instilled in you a strong need for external approval, causing you to mold yourself to others' expectations. Past experiences and painful memories may have made it difficult for you to trust people and let go of hurtful thoughts. Regardless of the circumstances, self-realization provides a safe space for healing and growth, enabling you to break free from the shackles of external influence.

How do you begin developing self-realization? Start by incorporating regular meditation into your daily routine. Make dedicated time for yourself every day. I understand that you might be thinking, "I don't have time for this!" However, if you have time to feel sorry for yourself, complain, check social media, or binge-watch TV, then you can surely spare time to invest in yourself, set goals, exercise, prioritize sleep, create a list of things you are grateful for, and work on personal growth.

About 40 percent of the activities that most people engage in daily are not conscious decisions but rather habitual behaviors. Among these habits, there are likely to be a handful of bad ones. However, by carefully observing your daily routines, you can easily transform a bad habit into a good one. The key is to introduce changes to your daily routines rather than trying to find extra time to do something new. Though these changes won't happen overnight, with time and practice, your dedication to self-improvement is crucial. However, by carefully observing your daily routines, you can easily transform a bad habit into a good one. The key is to introduce changes to your daily routines rather than trying to find extra time to do something new.

Remember, you are the main character of this story, not me, not them, but you. This is not an audition; it's up to you to carve out a unique place in this world that fits you perfectly. Follow your inspirations and joys, and give your life true meaning. You hold the power to heal. Whatever happened to you isn't your fault, but it's within your control to free yourself from the burdens of your past, to prevent it from stealing anything good from your future. While you can't control everything, you have the choice to orient yourself toward joy, well-being, healing, peace, calmness, and acceptance. Make your mind a place that uplifts you. Seek and find your community. Continuously shed old layers of yourself, grow, and evolve. Learn from the past, and assimilate the present into valuable lessons and new insights. It's all up to you. This is good news because it means you don't have anyone's permission to live life your way. Never outsource your power. Embrace the fact that you're the main character, and now is the time to take the lead.

Most of us know this deep inside, but sometimes, we can get so caught up in disappointments that we may forget it. That's why it is so important to set up reminders and make time to heal ourselves, prioritize self-care, and help others understand and respect this need.

Believe that happiness is a result of self-realization. It's essential to allow oneself to go through a process to experience genuine happiness. So, those are the phases I need to go through to get there:

- **Accept the pain.** It's essential to acknowledge your hardships and confront your situation. Denying or avoiding pain may seem like a path to happiness, but in reality, it's the opposite. Allow yourself to experience and process your pains.
- **Choose not to stay in pain.** This is the essence of "self-empowerment." You have the option to dwell on bitterness and helplessness or take action and empower yourself to handle the challenges. The choice is yours whether to live with or without pain.
- **Forgive yourself and other people.** Before extending forgiveness, consider that others may also be hurting when they cause pain. Recognize that you should see yourself for who you truly are, not as others may want you to be. Forgive not because they deserve it, but because you deserve inner peace. By doing so, you will find that happiness is no longer dependent on external factors but rather resides within you. It's about how you perceive things, and what you want, and this guides your choice to live your life authentically.
- **Take responsibility for your life.** Sometimes, we allow other people, circumstances, or past pains to control our lives. Consequently, we become unhappy and bitter, constantly blaming others for who we are, where we are, or how we should be. This cycle is exhausting as it perpetuates a pattern of blame. Instead, don't be preoccupied with what others think about you or the standards they set. Take charge of your life and choices.
- **Learn to let go and trust yourself.** Happiness involves learning to let go of expectations, whether they come from yourself or others. Realize that you can't always have things go your way. At work, for instance, you can't be certain that all your strategies will work out as planned. However, before letting go, cultivate a deeper trust in yourself.

- **Learn to receive blessings.** Take notice of the little things that bring you joy and the people who provide you with reassurance in your abilities. This is called receiving. Often, we have reasons to be happy, but we fail to recognize them, especially during times of sorrow or when we take them for granted. It's essential to open our eyes and hearts, realizing that the things that bring us happiness have been there all along.
- **Have somebody to turn to.** Even during challenging times, some people will support and uplift you. Yet, we sometimes remain surrounded by individuals who make us deeply unhappy. If you find yourself unhappy, seek out people who will nurture and support you, or consider finding a partner who will serve as a well-spring of inspiration.
- **Be hopeful.** Hope is more powerful than mere optimism because it's genuine and grounded in reality. Sometimes, optimism can be a way to deny hardship, where you appear positive on the surface but feel anxious inside. On the other hand, hope goes deeper; it allows you to look forward to the future despite recognizing the difficulties and pains. A truly hopeful person acknowledges the gravity of the situation and faces it head-on, knowing that it will eventually lead to positive outcomes. Hope doesn't deny difficulties; it embraces them while remaining optimistic about the future.
- **Keep the faith alive.** At times, you may face challenges that seem overwhelming, and handling them alone can be daunting. In such moments, draw strength from your belief in someone more powerful, who loves you deeply and will take care of you. Having faith, whether in a higher power or a greater purpose, can provide hope and comfort.
- **You can give intangible gifts even without your conscious effort.** People may later tell you that you've helped them, and gradually, you'll feel the difference you're making in their lives. That's a profound gift. When you assist others, their affirmations like, "You're good,"

resonate within you, and you come to realize that your goodness isn't solely tied to meeting deadlines or receiving a raise. It's about recognizing your inherent self-worth, being loved for who you truly are, and not just for the results you deliver or the money you contribute. This reinforces your positive attitude towards life's challenges.
- **Be grateful.** Cultivate a sense of gratitude within yourself. Take time to appreciate what you have. However, also acknowledge that there are opportunities to improve your life.
- **It's all in the mind.** Our happiness or unhappiness is often a result of our thoughts. Unhappy individuals may become attached to their unhappiness, resisting change. Negative thinking attracts more negative thoughts. If one constantly expects tragedy, they may inadvertently bring it upon themselves, unconsciously fulfilling their fears.
- **Money isn't everything.** While people may strive to accumulate wealth, the happiness that money can buy diminishes over time. Studies indicate that personal relationships, spirituality, and self-perception have a more direct impact on well-being than the amount of money one possesses.
- **Discover the best friend in you.** Positive change is possible for everyone. Find happiness within yourself by embracing the best friend that resides within you. Be authentic and avoid being overly critical of unattainable goals. Happiness lies within; it's time to stop searching for it outside of yourself.

Real happiness can withstand the challenge posed by external experiences. When you can endure the hurtful actions of others and still respond with love and forgiveness, and when you can maintain that inner peace despite the painful circumstances you encounter, then you will discover true happiness.

I recently reached this state of mind, and it has been a long journey. I have read many books, listened to podcasts, and conducted extensive research to come to this conclusion. Through inner work and self-reflection, I have reached a point in my life where I am the happiest I've ever been. The tips I discovered during this process have truly worked for me, and I hope they will also be beneficial to others.

I know that this is something within your control. The concept may sound easy, but the real challenge lies in changing our mindset. We must let go of the "victim mentality". You know what? I get it. It's much easier to blame our misery on others than to take responsibility for ourselves. It's like a safety blanket that gives us the sweet illusion that it's okay to feel this way. And you know what? It's okay to feel unhappy from time to time. However, it's also within our hands to do something about it.

Chapter 6: Don't lose yourself in someone else's dream

If we know all of this, why do we sometimes lose ourselves in relationships? This usually happens when you have a naturally giving personality and are eager to please your partner. You may find yourself constantly trying to meet their expectations and priorities, especially if you haven't yet discovered your purpose or passions. Additionally, the inability to say no and having conflicting expectations that go unmet by your partner can lead to disappointments. However, the primary reason for losing ourselves in relationships is often neglecting self-care and not investing enough time in nurturing ourselves.

Whatever the reason may be, the good news is that every individual has the potential to be creative and resourceful.

You possess the power within yourself to keep back from the chaotic snow globe of emotions and observe what is happening to you from an outside perspective.

Losing yourself in a moment and fully immersing yourself in the company of the one you love is one of the best feelings in life. Wanting to please your partner is natural, but it's essential to maintain your sense of self to avoid becoming codependent and potentially resentful. Have you noticed a pattern of trying to please your partner and then feeling irritated when they don't acknowledge your efforts? This reaction might indicate unresolved issues that need attention and healing. The fact you mentioned feeling bothered because you prioritize activities your partner enjoys suggests that there could be undressed wounds that require your consideration and care.

Whether you feel lost in a relationship or are afraid to start one, you may find yourself sacrificing your individuality when involved with narcissists and abusers. These individuals typically demand dominance, prioritize their needs above all else, and assert that they are always right.

Women, in particular, can be susceptible to losing themselves in relationships due to cultural conditioning. Even in healthy relationships, this tendency may arise from a place of love rather than fear. Slowly, and often imperceptibly, we compromise ourselves, unaware of the risks this poses to our well-being. Following a breakup, the sense of being lost can be devastating. Conversely, if we choose to stay in such relationships, we risk becoming empty shells, feeling powerless, anxious, or depressed. It's important to recognize that experiencing such emotions is normal, and many people go through similar situations. Frequently, power struggles arise, characterized by repeated, unresolved arguments whether centered around a single recurring issue or numerous trivial matters. These conflicts often revolve around questions of control, meeting needs, and intimacy levels.

Real intimacy becomes elusive when we don't feel safe. Avoiding intimacy and vulnerability can be a way to protect ourselves and maintain a sense of autonomy. The fear of becoming close to our partner may stem from concerns about dependency being unsafe. It's not uncommon for some individuals to feel unsafe both within and outside of relationships. The more threatened we feel by both intimacy and independence, the greater the conflict within the relationship. A common story we often hear from couples is, "When I'm single, I'm living my best life. But then I meet someone...and I end up losing myself in the relationship." This pattern highlights the struggle between finding joy and fulfillment on one's own versus the challenges of maintaining a sense of self within a partnership.

Yes, we humans are usually quite adept at prioritizing ourselves when we're alone. However, when a lover enters and steals the spotlight, they often become the center of attention. I say "steal", because, in reality, we willingly offer them our focus and care. We are more than happy to give our all, showering them and the relationship with love and attention. Yet, as time goes, by, we may find ourselves looking around and realizing that we have entirely lost our sense of self within the relationship.

Losing yourself in a relationship means that your attention is so intensely focused on your partner that you start to lose touch with your own identity. Your life no longer feels completely your own, and you struggle to maintain a sense of self separated from your partner. This can manifest practically as a passion project left half-finished in the back of a cupboard, months passing without seeing your best friends, and a decline in prioritizing your career, hobbies, or interests as you once did. Your unique sparkle, that special YOU-ness that defines who you are, seems to have faded away. And this feeling is far from pleasant.

Within a relationship, there is an innate desire to feel loved and accepted, which often leads to sacrificing parts of ourselves to achieve that acceptance or maintain harmony. Unless you consciously strive to maintain a separate sense of self, this tendency can cause you to lose your identity.

We gradually lose ourselves in small ways. It might begin with the excitement of romance, where it's normal to want to please our loved ones and spend a significant amount of time together. However, emotionally mature adults don't completely abandon their activities or give up their lives because they have their interests and pursuits. They also don't overlook improper behavior from their partner solely due to strong physical attraction. Moreover, they are not desperate to be in a relationship or to hold onto one at any cost.

Many people do well on their own, but once they enter a relationship, they may start losing their autonomy, avoiding conflicts, and prioritizing pleasing their partner. In the presence of intense "chemistry," they may overlook negative indicators that could be warning signs not to get involved. Feel-good chemicals in our brain can alleviate feelings of emptiness, leading us to crave more of that emotional high. Consequently, we become reluctant to let go of these pleasurable sensations, especially if we were unhappy being alone, as it makes us more vulnerable to holding on.

Hence, we become increasingly dependent on our loved ones, potentially neglecting our friendships and altering our routines to spend more time with our partners. Particularly, for women, work and professional goals might take a backseat in the relationship.

The desire to please our partner can escalate into obsession. The strong need for connection might cause us to deny or overlook concerning behaviors displayed by our partner and even question our perceptions. Consequently, boundaries become blurred, leading us to adopt our partner's point of view more readily.

If our partner is abusive, our self-doubt grows, and our self-esteem diminishes. We find it challenging to say "no" or set limits on what we're willing to do or accept from them. Additionally, confusion arises between what our partner's emotions and our feelings. We start feeling responsible for our emotions, especially if we're being blamed. If they're sad, we feel sad too. This confusion can lead us to lose touch with our beliefs, values, and opinions. Often, we may not even realize this until we become deeply involved in a serious relationship. In the process, we may willingly give up our hobbies, outside interests, friends, and sometimes even relationships with our relatives. Initially, we might do this willingly, especially at the start of the relationship. However, later on, we may comply with our partner's wishes. Although our choices may seem desirable or necessary, we are often not consciously aware of the price we pay: our sense of self.

This pattern reflects a "lost self." When our identity is primarily defined by external references, we repeatedly prioritize our relationships over our own well-being, rather than occasionally, which would be normal. In important relationships, we develop a fear of losing connection with others or their approval. This leads us to repeatedly sacrifice ourselves in both small and significant ways. These sacrifices range from insignificant concessions to giving up a career, cutting off relatives, or even condoning or participating in unethical behavior that we would have considered unimaginable before.

Over the years, a pattern of compliance develops, and new norms are established. Gradually, guilt, anger, and resentment build up often in silence. We start blaming ourselves for the situation. Our self-esteem, autonomy, and self-respect, which we had when entering the relationship, are slowly eroded. As a result, we may experience increased anxiety and depression, and our behaviors might become more obsessive or compulsive. The sense of choice and freedom we once had diminishes until we feel trapped and hopeless, with our feelings of depression and despair growing. In some cases, we might even develop an addiction or physical symptoms. Eventually, we can turn into a mere shadow of our former selves.

These symptoms are intensified in authoritarian relationships, where decisions primarily revolve around the needs and authority of one person. Such dynamics are common in abusive relationships, where our partner makes explicit demands. When our partner is insistent, it feels as though we are forced to choose between ourselves and the relationship, and we may feel compelled to sacrifice ourselves to maintain it. Consequently, we start to feel invisible, no longer viewed as separate individuals with independent needs and desires, assuming we knew what they were. To please our partner and avoid conflicts, we give them up and our own needs and inadvertently collude in sacrificing our sense of self.

Our relationship might be with an addict or someone who has a mental illness or a personality disorder, such as narcissistic, borderline, or antisocial personality disorder. These partners can be manipulative and may exhibit abusive behavior, or they may threaten abuse or abandonment when they don't get their way or sense that we're becoming independent. Any action we take toward asserting autonomy, such as setting boundaries, threatens their sense of control. They will attempt to maintain power and authority using tactics like guilt-tripping, character assassinations, gas-lighting, and all forms of criticism and emotional abuse.

This pattern may have been established in childhood and carried over into our adult relationships. As a result, we find ourselves walking on eggshells and living in fear, which can traumatize our nervous systems, leading to symptoms that persist even after we leave such relationships. Seeking outside support and counseling is essential in such cases.

Healthy relationships are interdependent, involving mutual give and take, respect for each other's needs and feelings, and the ability to settle conflict through authentic communication. Decisions and problem-solving are collaborative, assertiveness plays a key role. Negotiations are not seen as a zero-sum game, and boundaries are expressed directly without hinting, manipulation, or expecting our partner to read our minds. In a healthy relationship, neither security nor autonomy is threatened by closeness. The vulnerability strengthens us instead of making us weaker. We can be more intimate and open when our autonomy and boundaries are intact and respected.

Both partners feel secure in their relationship. They value and support each other's separateness and independence, without feeling threatened by their partner's autonomy. This supportive dynamic allows the relationship to nurture and encourage their individual growth, providing them with the courage to explore their talents and personal development.

Fortunately, it is possible to recover our lost sense of self and escape a narcissist-codependent trap. The first step is to shift our focus away from trying to change our partner and instead look within ourselves for change. It's easy to get trapped in denial for years, hoping that our partner will change, but real change starts from within. When we make positive changes in ourselves, our partner may respond positively as well, or regardless of their response, we will feel better and stronger because we've grown in self-respect.

My Own Identity: An Introduction to Self-Discovery

Losing yourself in a relationship is far from a personal failing. It's a natural aspect of emotionally committed relationships. Problems are, in reality, unrecognized processes of growth within the context of the partnership. In other words, losing oneself in a relationship is an almost inevitable experience, and it can mark the beginning of a profoundly empowering journey of personal development.

With the right approach, there is no need to end a relationship to find yourself again. Rediscovering yourself while still in a relationship can lead to the development of a more secure sense of self, reducing the likelihood of losing oneself in the future.

The only time when ending a relationship is necessary is if it becomes abusive or controlling. It can be challenging to change the status quo and ensure safety. If you find yourself in an abusive relationship, seeking professional help from a psychologist is essential.

In recovery, you will find hope as the focus shifts from the other person to yourself, where change is possible. Work on raising your self-esteem and learn to express your feelings, wants, and needs, as well as setting healthy boundaries. Developing positive self-care habits will be crucial. Eventually, your happiness and self-esteem won't depend on others anymore. You will gain the capacity for both autonomy and intimacy, experiencing your power and self-love. You will feel expansive and creative, able to generate and pursue your own goals. It's important to note that these patterns won't automatically disappear if you leave an unhealthy relationship; recovery requires ongoing maintenance. Psychotherapy can be beneficial in healing from PTSD, childhood trauma, and internalized or toxic shame. Over time, changes in thinking and behavior will become more natural, and the tools and skills learned will become new, healthy habits. Remember, perfectionism is a symptom of shame, and there is no such thing as perfect recovery. Recurring symptoms merely present ongoing opportunities for learning and growth!

After this, you will never lose yourself in a relationship. Love your partner fiercely, but always follow your unique dreams and desires. Be true to yourself.

All my previous relationships drained me. Not only because I was with the wrong men and kept trying to make things work where there was no way, but also because I was the type of person who justified, accommodated, and compromised. I accommodated men because I wanted to be liked and avoid rejection. I justified their lousy behavior because I wanted to be in a relationship and not be alone. I would compromise my values and romantic ideals just to have someone in my life. On the surface, I was an independent woman, strong, fierce, and full of energy and opinions. However, when it came to relationships, I'd lose my power and myself in them. I would become a meek mouse with no voice or opinions, putting their needs first and ignoring my own. I kept quiet about how I felt and wouldn't question things. It took me a few attempts to recognize my unhealthy patterns.

Firstly, I was subconsciously copying the behavior of my grandmother and mother, who needed to survive with my despotic grandfather and father in a very turbulent relationship. I didn't know any better until I learned the hard way.

Secondly, I didn't feel worthy of love. I didn't believe I was good enough for anyone, and I was afraid to be myself, as I didn't feel like I had much to offer.

Thirdly, I wasn't happy with myself and my life, and I believed a relationship would change that, so my desire to be in one was pretty strong.

These patterns made me feel and act like I was desperate for love. Once I found myself with someone, I'd do anything to please them and keep them in my life.

I used to be a cheerful giver. I would shoulder all the responsibility in the relationship myself. I made their life easier by constantly doing things for them, sometimes at the expense of my well-being. I accommodated their busy schedules, moods, and problems. I worked to boost their self-esteem and improve their lifestyle, hoping it would bring them greater happiness. However, in the process, I completely lost myself in these relationships.

Everything in my relationships resolved around them. They become my main focus and the most important aspect of my life.

I would neglect myself, losing my own identity in the name of love. My top priority was to keep them happy, believing it would keep the relationship. However, no amount of crazy giving and accommodating could salvage dysfunctional relationships. As a result, when these relationships inevitably ended, I found myself with nothing left to give. Each breakup left me feeling empty as if a little part of me had died with every failed connection. I had become so consumed by the relationship that I had completely neglected my well-being, and this felt incredibly unhealthy and intoxicating. Eventually, I started to become more aware of these harmful patterns and their impact on my love life. It led me to make some promises to myself:
1. The relationship with myself comes first.
2. I will always love myself more than any other significant other.

Although they might sound a bit harsh, these rules have served me and my relationship amazingly well so far.

The truth is, your relationship with yourself is the most important one in your life. It is also the foundation of any other relationship, so it makes sense to prioritize and nurture it.

If you love someone else more than yourself, you will always compromise too much, ignore the red flags, get hurt, and lose yourself in your relationships. You can't love healthily unless you love yourself first. This fact is widely acknowledged because it holds true. Moreover, loving yourself will help you set stronger boundaries in relationships, protect yourself, and find the courage to walk away from any relationship that doesn't serve you.

Along with these promises, I also made a decision that I wanted to create something different in my love life. I aimed to create a healthy and happy relationship, unlike the ones my parents and grandparents had, or the ones I had experienced in the past.

To achieve this, I knew I needed to evolve and become a braver, more authentic version of myself within my relationships.

Firstly, I took a break from dating and focused on finding greater happiness and inner strength.

Secondly, as I opened myself up to new relationships, I established some new personal boundaries to ensure I remained strong within my relationship. I didn't want to lose myself again, because honestly, losing oneself is far more painful than losing a relationship. It takes a considerable amount of time to regain one's strength, dignity, and sense of truth.

Here are some things I did differently before and after entering a new relationship, which you can do to ensure you don't lose yourself.

Firstly, establish a strong foundation while you are single. We often lose ourselves in relationships because we don't feel worthy of love, and our boundaries are weak. Unresolved past traumas can affect our internal thoughts and trigger irrational behavior at times. When you love yourself, you gain clarity on how you want to feel and who you want to be in your next relationship. Setting healthy boundaries is crucial, as it prevents you from losing your identity within a relationship. So, how do you start loving yourself?

Here are three tips you can implement straight away:
1. Start every day by asking yourself: What do I need today? How can I love myself today? Follow the answers, as they will help you be more loving and respectful towards

yourself and others. Do something nice for yourself every day.
2. Operate from a loving, compassionate place within yourself. Choose people, situations, and things in your life that support you and don't harm you. Honor your own needs and feelings. Be kind to yourself and stop judging yourself. Set powerful boundaries to protect your time and energy. Become your cheerleader and listen to your intuition.
3. Change your priorities. Put yourself first, and everything else comes after. Choose yourself and make your well-being a priority. Acknowledge your importance in your way.

When you start following the path of self-love, you will show up differently in your life and relationships.

Secondly, know who you are. Know your needs, desires, dreams, values, and priorities. Essentially, know yourself deeply. This knowledge will prevent you from compromising too much in a relationship. Your strong sense of self will help you stay true to what truly matters to you. As a result, you will experience a sense of security that comes from within, not solely from your relationship.

I have two little exercises that will help you get to know and understand yourself and your needs better:
1. Create a list of your current needs. Grab a piece of paper and create four columns. Title each column: emotional, mental, physical, and spiritual. Take your time and explore what you need in these four categories to feel fulfilled.
2. Write down your top five to ten priorities. These are the things that are important to you, that you'd like to focus on right now. List them in order of importance.

These exercises will give you a stronger sense of direction in life and help you explore what is truly important to you. It's sensible to revisit them occasionally since things will likely change over time.

Your needs will be different a few months down the line, and your priorities will also evolve, as we are constantly growing and changing. The goal isn't to define yourself in rigid terms, but to understand what you need and want at this point in your life.

Thirdly, have strong boundaries. Know your non-negotiables in relationships. The things you won't tolerate, the things you don't want to compromise on, and the things you don't want in your relationship. Communicate them clearly so your partner knows and respects your limits.

Chapter 7: Set up healthy boundaries

Healthy boundaries will make you feel stronger and more empowered in your next relationship. If you don't honor your boundaries, you will feel exhausted, overwhelmed, and drained. Healthy boundaries prevent you from losing yourself in love. The health of your communication defines healthy relationships. Understanding your partner's boundaries will transform your ability to communicate and help address issues before they overwhelm you.

Healthy boundaries are a reflection of the principles, rules, and guidelines you have set for yourself. A breach of those boundaries occurs when your partner disrespects, ignores, or isn't aware of those principles of your personal needs.

Having a lack of boundaries can often lead to emotional manipulation from your significant other, whether intentional or not. You may find it challenging to say no when someone asks you for a favor, or you might be uncomfortable with public displays of affection. If this is the case, it's essential to speak up and communicate these needs to your partner. Learn to recognize the signs that someone has crossed your boundaries, which may include feelings of anger, resentment, or guilt.

The conversation you may have with your partner might be tough at first, but it can be the key to a happy relationship. There are many types of boundaries in relationships, including those within marriage, which can establish better communication and intimacy. Some conversations may be easier than others, but it's better to address them with preparation rather than during tense moments after an argument. It may also be helpful to seek the guidance of a personal therapist to discern where you most need boundaries. So, I am going to provide some examples of emotional boundaries to get you started.
1. **Saying No.** You may find it easier to sacrifice your own needs for your partner out of fear of upsetting them.

However, if they ask something of you that goes against your principles, disrespects your time, or forces you to sacrifice something important, it's okay to say no. It doesn't have to be harsh but learn to say it assertively. One way to say "No" is to state, I don't think it aligns with my journey today. I am not feeling drawn to that, so I'll pass. My journey is leading this way, not that way. You can use different variations of this approach, but the key is to be respectful yet firm. Many times, I've used this method, and nobody got offended.
2. **Refusing to take the blame.** Sometimes your partner may place the blame on you out of hurt or guilt. However, it's essential to remember that their anger or actions are not your fault. Do not let them manipulate your emotions or avoid taking responsibility. Acknowledge their pain, let them know you are there for them, but assert that you will not accept blame for their actions.
3. **Expecting respect.** You deserve kindness and loving communication. If you feel your partner is expressing unjustified anger or using a disrespectful tone, you have every right to remove yourself from the scenario. Let them know that if they want to have a conversation, it must come from a place of respect.
4. **Dictating your feelings.** When you're part of a couple, opinions and emotions can sometimes feel blurred. Learn to distinguish your feelings from your partner's and their perception of your emotions. If they speak for you, kindly correct them and kindly ask them not to dictate your emotions.
5. **Finding your identity outside of the relationship.** Codependency can lead to a merging of identities, where "I" becomes "we," and "you" may get lost in the mix. Remember that you are not just one half of a whole; you are your own person with passions, interests, and vibrant intelligence. It's okay to have a sense of self that is separate from your partner.
6. **Accepting help.** Some people are more independent and may find it difficult to rely on their partners during tough

times. If you need help, it's essential to establish your boundaries and communicate what you do and do not assist with. For example, you may ask for help with finances but prefer space when dealing with family issues. Striking this balance can be a delicate tango, but open communication leads to a smoother rhythm.

7. **Asking for space.** Sometimes we just need to be alone during the emotional upheaval. However, in a relationship, it might feel like you are never alone. Asking for space may seem to your partner like you are pushing them away, even if that's not your intention.
8. **Communicating discomfort.** Whether your partner tells a hurtful joke or crosses a physical line, learning to articulate your discomfort clearly will help in setting your boundaries. Let them know what you will not tolerate, and plan a course of action for crossing that boundary. Phrases like "Please don't do that; it makes me uncomfortable" or "I don't like it when you (ex: use that word, touch me there, use that tone)" are clear and concise.
9. **Sharing mutually.** It's okay to take things slowly at the beginning of a relationship. Don't feel pressured to share everything upfront or believe that you have to share first for your significant other to open up. Vulnerability should be mutual, with both partners checking in and creating a safe space for sharing.
10. **Sticking up for yourself.** In an argument, you or your partner may say things you regret that are mean or hurtful. Establish that you won't accept being spoken to in such a way. You have intrinsic worth and deserve to be spoken to kindly. Make it known that you need an apology and that you need your partner to acknowledge the hurt their words have caused.
11. **Choosing to be vulnerable.** Vulnerability should not be demanded. While it is an important component of a healthy relationship, you should never feel pressured to open up about difficult topics at any stage of your relationship. You can share your feelings and experiences on your terms. You

should feel safe to communicate that you may need time to discuss specific topics or memories.
12. **Your right to privacy.** There are various levels of privacy in a relationship. For example, you may share a home computer but keep your email password to yourself. This choice is reasonable. Your belongings, thoughts, texts, journal entries, and even topics as significant as past relationships or traumas are yours to share or not to share at your discretion. Infringement on those boundaries is not acceptable.
13. **The ability to change your mind.** Your choices are your decisions, and you have the right to make new ones if you wish. If you change your mind, your partner should not make you feel guilty about it. Be clear with your reasoning or simply state that you decided to change your mind. Of course, being open is important, but it should happen on your terms.
14. **You're right to your own time.** You get to dictate where and with whom you spend your time, whether alone or apart. If you don't enjoy going to Monday night football, establish that Monday nights are your alone time or your weekly wine night with your pals. Perhaps you need to be by yourself for a few days after a big fight; you are within your right to ask for that.
15. **The need to handle negative energy.** A personal boundary can also be one that you set for your behavior. It is important to navigate unhealthy anger and resentment so you don't bring negative energy into a shared space. If you can't handle it on your own, ask for help. Share your negative emotions and lighten those toxic feelings by being honest about your mood.
16. **The freedom to express spiritual boundaries.** Your beliefs are your own, regardless of how much you may or may not have in common with your partner in terms of spirituality or religion. Both you and your significant other should respect each other's beliefs, foster and encourage each other's spiritual growth, and be open to learning about each other's culture or faith.

17. **The right to remain true to your principles.** Set a boundary with yourself so that your principles remain intact, regardless of who you are dating. Of course, you can change your mind as your conversations with your partner open new doors to new ideas. However, you shouldn't feel pressured to adopt their stances out of fear of upsetting them.
18. **The ability to communicate physical needs.** Learn to communicate what your body needs. Are you an early riser who needs to be in bed before 10:00 pm? Then make sure your partner respects your physical needs by not making loud noises or watching TV late into the evening. On the other hand, take the time to understand your significant other's boundaries. If they prefer a later bedtime, work out an arrangement rather than pressuring them to go to sleep before their biological clock allows them to.
19. **Your right to your material possessions.** Deciding what to share and what to keep for yourself is never an easy task. Some couples open joint bank accounts, while others prefer financial independence. Material and financial boundaries are commonplace in every relationship.
20. **Your ability to manage your own time.** Another important relationship boundary to set for yourself is learning to manage your time in a way that doesn't disrespect your significant other. When you're single, you can put off doing the dishes as long as you want. However, in a relationship, your time is not just your own. If you agree to date at 8:00 pm, it's essential to stick to your word.

It's one thing to know what your boundaries are, but it's a whole different ball game to establish them, especially if that means unlearning bad habits. Try to avoid reacting with anger when setting boundaries. Often, we don't fully realize our boundaries until someone crosses them. However, there are better ways to communicate your boundaries to your partner.

Here are some thoughts on establishing your boundaries in a relationship:

- Find a calm moment: If your partner crosses a boundary, take some time to work through your anger, ensuring safety and preserving your health. Give yourself space to reflect, and write down what disturbed you. Define the boundary clearly, and wait until a peaceful moment to have a conversation.
- Be assertive: State your boundaries clearly and effectively. Make it known that you will not tolerate any crossing of that boundary, and explain why it bothers you.
- Be loving: Avoid threatening your partner or speaking out of anger. Let him or her know that you are setting your boundaries out of trust and love for both of you.
- Reciprocate: Be sure to ask your partner what boundaries they need to establish, and do your best to honor them. Model the behavior you want to see in your partner. Communication is the key here.

It may be scary to be vulnerable and admit what you need from your significant other, but you know yourself and your needs better than anyone else.

A loving partner, the partner you deserve, will respect and value the boundaries you have set.

Ultimately, you will find yourselves closer than ever. Showing your loved ones that you are willing to set boundaries will encourage them to share their boundaries with you. It may take time and hard work, but the best things always do. Healthy boundaries will make you feel stronger and more empowered in your next relationship. If you don't honor your boundaries, you will feel exhausted, overwhelmed, and drained. Healthy boundaries prevent you from losing yourself in love.

Another important aspect is having your friends. It's very easy to get infatuated with a new relationship, become deeply involved, and forget about the world outside. While this is a natural part of every new relationship, don't neglect your friends. Schedule

regular time with them. They've been your rock and sounding board many times and can continue to be so. Don't limit your life to just your new partner. You need other perspectives and support.
It is also important to have your own life. Just because you are in a relationship doesn't mean you need to give up the things you love doing, even if you feel tempted, especially at the beginning when things are exciting, and you want to spend as much time with the person as possible. It's important to maintain your normal routine as much as you can. Make time for the things you love doing and prioritize them because they contribute to your happiness, making them just as important as your relationship. Keep some hobbies that you only do on your own or with people other than your partner. Plan some time every week when you engage in activities separately. Schedule solo dates, cultivate a spiritual practice, and stick to your exercise routine.

Doing things on your own will help you stay connected to yourself and cultivate a sense of self. It will also keep your relationship fresh. No relationship can fulfill all your needs and desires. That is why you need different things in your life, apart from your relationship, to keep you growing and expanding in new directions. Additionally, the time spent on your own will help you nurture your relationship with yourself and keep your independence.

Stay true to yourself. Don't suddenly change who you are for someone else. For example, don't pretend to be a football lover just because your boyfriend likes football, or don't force yourself to go shopping with your girlfriend just to please her. Be honest with yourself and communicate what you like and what you don't like with your partner.

Also, make some independent decisions. You don't need to consult your partner about every single decision. Express your opinions, share your thoughts, speak your mind, and tell them how you feel. All of these will help your partner to understand you better.

Communicate openly. Talk about how you feel, discuss what isn't working for you, and share your likes and dislikes. You can even express your fear of losing yourself in the relationship again to your new partner. Honest and open communication will only bring you closer. Improving a relationship is possible when you know what is not working. So, talk openly!

Stop over-giving and accommodating. Over-giving usually stems from not recognizing your value and seeking approval. We often believe that the more we give, the more love we will receive from our partner. Unfortunately, it doesn't work like that. In the long run, over-giving is a sure way to increase resentment and feel taken for granted. Resentment can significantly impact the happiness and longevity of a relationship. So, when you over-give, you not only risk losing yourself in the relationship but also jeopardize the relationship itself.

Reflect on your relationships. How you felt, how you compromised, how you betrayed yourself. Our previous relationships can provide valuable insights about ourselves. Therefore, examine the mistakes you have made in the past and learn from them. Decide what you don't want to repeat and what you want to do differently in your next relationship. Commit to staying strong and true to yourself.

Set the rules that you are going to follow once you meet someone. You can use the ones I created for myself or create your own!

Chapter 8: Beliefs and values shape our identity

Know your values. You may not be aware of it, you may not be conscious of it, but your values shape your decisions, and your decisions shape your life. Your values signal what is important to you. They are emotional states that show you what is important and what you want to experience.

Creating and stating your values consciously can change the direction of your life. Here are some values that I believe make life more valuable and meaningful:

Health and Energy: Great health gives you energy and vitality, enabling you to delve deeper into the more important things in life and give more energy and time to those you love. Make the value of health and energy a priority in life by learning what daily nutrition and exercise are best to fuel your body.

Love: Making love a priority in life means there is no room for hate or indifference.

Gratitude and appreciation: It costs you nothing, but makes you so rich. It takes nothing away from anyone else but gives you so much power.

Kindness and compassion: Have you noticed how good it feels when you are kind to someone for no reason? It feels good to be kind because it is right to be kind.

Integrity: When you value integrity, you value doing what is right. It is such a powerful value that not only makes a difference in your own life but also sets a powerful example for all those around you. It brings honesty and trust.

Growth: Growth comes from experiences, learning, failures, achievements, and intention. The intention is to become better.

This doesn't mean to get better just to "win"; it means getting better so you can contribute more to the world and experience more joy and fulfillment.

Giving: This ties to kindness and compassion. As humans, we are built to give. Not just giving money or things, but giving ourselves fully to others in need, serving selflessly. You give because it is in your nature. It's not an effort; it is natural, feels good, and you know there is no lack. Although, you need to be careful to whom and when you give. As many can abuse your kindness and giving nature.

Peace: Ahhh, peace. Nothing more needs to be said. It's about reaching that place of needing nothing, being content alone, and experiencing bliss. It's about presence, the silence at the peak of the mountain.

Family, friendship, and connection: It's about giving your complete presence to the people you love, and even to some strangers, and building that connection. It's making someone else's day better just because you were in it. It's bringing your best self to every encounter so the other person walks away with a smile.

Happiness: It's joy. It's that playfulness and sense of fun. It's experiencing a state of real happiness, where time seems to stop, and you love what you are doing. It's an internal state and a choice. It's always available and never on sale. You decide to make this a priority and a top value.

Knowing what your values are can also help you find job opportunities that align most with your deeply held beliefs and can boost your confidence during an interview. If you strongly believe in security, you might look for a position where your duties are unlikely to change too often, where you work the same hours each day, and your work environment remains consistent. On the other hand, if you value stimulation, you might seek a position that involves frequent travel and where duties vary from day to day.

As you enter adulthood, understanding more about your values can help you become prepared to make decisions for yourself and inspire you to become the person you'd like to be as you embark on your career. I value communication, and I love learning about it every day. Additionally, I value people, which influenced my decision to find a job in a non-profit organization where I can integrate my love for communication into my career. Similarly, writing is another form of communication that brings me great enjoyment.

Understanding the things you value most has the potential to help you better handle stressful situations that can sometimes impair your ability to solve problems and make decisions. When you're facing a challenging situation, consider how you can use your values to make a choice.

It may be tempting to quickly react to a certain situation, but spending a few minutes reflecting on your values instead can help ensure that the choice you make is the most practical and truly aligns with what you value. For example, if you strongly value selflessness and encounter a person who needs help, helping that person can make you feel good about yourself because you were able to directly demonstrate your selflessness.

By identifying a few of your most important values, you can better focus on what matters most to you and remove the things in your life that aren't as meaningful or don't align with who you are and what you want to become. To identify these values, pay extra attention to the choices you make every day and take note of the things that are most important to you. As you gain a deeper understanding of your values, you may find that your time becomes more meaningful.

Healthy relationships are created by two strong and complete individuals who can exist without each other. Healthy relationships are free of codependency, and it starts with yourself. The stronger your relationship with yourself, the less likely you will lose your sense of self in your next relationship.

You can build strong foundations now by getting to know yourself, exploring life on your own, and establishing habits that make you happy. Learn about your values and beliefs. When you feel strong within and meet the right person, you will stay grounded throughout the initial phase of dating and have better judgment. You will maintain a strong identity, make wiser romantic choices, and avoid heartache. You will understand your fears, and what triggers them, and develop deep self-awareness, making everything clearer.

Have you ever wondered what fuels your motivations and drives your attitudes and behavior? You'd like to think it's all a conscious decision and the result of in-depth rationalization on your part. There's truth to that, but many other levers inside of you that act subconsciously. Among those, two fundamental concepts live at the root of everything. If you understand what these are, you can not only comprehend yourself and what is holding you back in life, but even scratch the surface of understanding the world and its behavior, at least since the rise of consciousness. So, what drives our attitude and behavior at the most basic level? It's our beliefs and values.

Our beliefs are the things we hold, regardless of whether we have any proof or objective truth. Beliefs are developed and inherited. As we grow up, we learn and adopt the views of those around us, especially those whom we look up to; parents, teachers, mentors, and colleagues. They all pass their beliefs on to us, and we have the choice to accept them or not. Over time, we might internalize them as our own beliefs or reject them. We also develop beliefs based on personal experiences and the emotions we associate with those moments. Furthermore, beliefs can form through our repeated actions. For example, if you are consistently late, you might start to believe that you are terrible at time management, when in fact, improving your alarm and sleep habits could change that perception. Gradually, beliefs shape our identity, and we become influenced by them to some extent. Here are some examples of beliefs that you might recognize: "God has created the world," "If a black cat crosses in front of you, something horrific will happen," and "Man has evolved from primates." As you may notice, some of these beliefs have science behind them, while others do not. Scientific research has constantly changed people's options over time by providing evidence to the contrary. Think about ideas such as the Earth being flat and the Sun revolving around the Earth. At some point, people believed that. Later on, science proved that they were not true, and most people stopped believing in them.

Regardless of the level of scientific or empirical proof, most people have difficulty justifying their beliefs, and frankly, most of us don't even like to. We would all be a lot happier if everyone else around us had the same beliefs as we do, or at least, if they would not challenge us on them. Of course, that is impossible, and this is precisely what fuels most of the world's conflicts.

Beliefs about ourselves. Things such as "I am smart," "I am stupid," "I am unlucky," "I am beautiful," and "I am strong"—are the ones that drive or stifle our motivation. They could be limiting beliefs (e.g., "I can't," "I'm not good at...," "I just don't have...") or they could be empowering (e.g., "I can," "I do").

Beliefs about ourselves develop during childhood and are closely related to the environment in which we grew up. Individuals who grew up in a close, supportive family who regularly encouraged them will probably develop a sense of self-confidence, though this is not a universal rule.

The way different people internalize these environment-driven beliefs or reject them also depends on their personalities. People with a naturally questioning mind and curiosity about the world will not blindly accept the beliefs of those around them. Similarly, people with a strong sense of self will not simply adopt what they are told about themselves. Instead, they will develop their self-image by analyzing their strengths and weaknesses.

What we believe to be true about ourselves, in fact, our self-image. These are the stories we tell ourselves, and over time, we become those stories. The beliefs become ingrained into our character, and we begin to filter everything through them. Our speech, body language, and emotional expressions are all influenced, one way or another, by those beliefs.

"I'm a procrastinator." "I'm just a bad speller."

You see, over time, beliefs can become labels. We plaster them on our foreheads and use them to justify our actions or inaction. They serve as mental pacifiers to allow us to maintain the status quo. Instead of learning how to spell, it's much easier to label yourself as a lousy speller.

Instead of learning how to manage time, labeling yourself as a procrastinator gives you a convenient carte blanche to maintain your existing behavior.

Interestingly enough, an objective fact might turn into a positive or negative belief depending on the person. For instance, you might be the tallest kid in your class, which would is a fact, but you can interpret it as an advantage or a disadvantage. That belief will then drive how you behave, as you perceive it as either damning or empowering.

Another type of belief is about others. These beliefs are usually ingrained into our minds by our mentors and parents (such as believing that a certain group of people is evil, unlike us who are all saints).

In contrast, some beliefs are developed based on our own experiences. For example, if a police officer mistreated you one time, you might develop a belief that all police are unfair. More extreme experiences can even lead to the development of phobias. These beliefs influence our attitudes and behavior toward others.

You don't have to look far to see the effects our beliefs about others have upon the world. Think about politics and religion, where the polarization of ideas generates powerful opinions about the "other" side. More often than not, those ideas morph into actions, oftentimes aggressive. Of course, the assumptions about others are also a result and a projection of our beliefs about ourselves. If you think of yourself as unlucky because you haven't had success in your career, you might conclude that anyone else who is successful is, in fact, lucky. Replace "lucky" with any other adjective, and you can see how easily you might morph the thing that you believe you don't have into an opinion about those who have it. Action, then, is only a few steps behind.

Beliefs about life and the world, such as "life sucks," "everything is terrible," or just the opposite, "the world is full of possibilities," are all beliefs we develop about the outside world. We formulate such beliefs about our closest world (like our home or street) up to humanity as a whole. Although we are not proud to admit it, we secretly compartmentalize the world into little boxes, and we have beliefs about each one of them. Of course, our opinion about a group of people is relative to our situation and context.

People in high socio-economic environments might think that people in low socio-economic backgrounds do not work hard enough. The latter group might think that the former had everything handed to them on a platter. Although these thoughts are objectively true, they are mostly not. We develop these biases toward the world because of an innate need to justify our place in it.

While beliefs about others and the world generate our stereotypes and can lead to xenophobia, racism, and sexism, or the literal opposite of all of those, beliefs about ourselves drive our self-image. Together, they set the boundaries of what and with whom we feel comfortable speaking, acting, helping, or asking for help. The gap between our beliefs about others and ourselves creates our attitude and eventually shapes our beliefs about our world in general.

Think: I am always unlucky, but everyone else around me is always lucky. I am a decent person; however, I am surrounded by people with hidden agendas. You can see how those thoughts, combined, might shape different types of attitudes in your mind. These thoughts could lead to cynicism and misanthropy or kindness and charity. It all depends on the direction in which those beliefs take you. And here comes the kicker: you can decide the direction you take. Your beliefs do not control you, so long as you become self-aware and take the help of your life.

If beliefs are things that we believe to be true, values are the compass in life that tell us what is right and what is wrong. Our values are often derived from our beliefs, but not always. Values set our standards for what we would and would not be prepared to do, in other words, what we think is important. However, note that values do not directly drive our actions; they simply guide us on what is right and wrong.

Some root-level values are easy to understand just by their name, such as honesty, health, and love. Although different people might define them differently, those definitions will be somewhat close. Other values are more difficult to define objectively because they mean vastly different things to different people. For instance, think about the value of success.

An entire system of values is like a living organism, and the importance you place on each of them affects the others around you. For instance, a person who values honesty and success might not sacrifice honesty for success if they hold honesty higher in their hierarchy. But what if things were reversed? At which point would the value of success push you to override the value of honesty? Look into politics and business, and you'll find an answer.

Similarly, if you hold the value of fitness higher than the value of health, you might do things toward your fitness that could damage your health. For that, see professional athletes who sacrifice their health for accolades.

In any country's political system, you can see the set of values at play in the candidates' platforms. An individual who values a social hierarchy based exclusively on financial meritocracy might prioritize economic growth over social welfare.

Note that values don't always have to be positive. Many of them are negative, but self-awareness to essential to realize whether we embody them. Consider anger, blame, and dishonesty, just to name a few. For example, Hitler and Stalin had values, but the application of their value system resulted in genocide.

If values serve as our compass, then morals act as the positive compass for society. This implies that by discarding negative values and embracing the positive ones, and subsequently having a group of people endorse them, we establish moral values or the values of a society.

Unlike morals, which are created by a group of people to maintain the sanctity of society, ethics take it one step further. Ethics consist of rules or norms that must be explicitly defined, stating what individuals must adhere to if they wish to gain acceptance. Codes of ethics serve as prime examples of these rules. Various professions, companies, and countries establish these ethical codes to uphold minimum standards applicable to all.

These are explicit rules that delineate what is considered good and bad. Moreover, ethical standards may result in punishments when disregarded. For instance, if you encounter a sign that says, "Do not litter," that represents an ethical rule. To behave ethically, you would refrain from throwing your garbage on the ground. Failing to do so may lead to a fin. On the other hand, if you come across a candy wrapper on the ground, discarded by someone else, you have no ethical obligation to pick it up. However, you do have a moral obligation to do so. If your set of values aligns with your society's moral values, you will likely pick up the wrapper and dispose of it properly in the garbage.

Your beliefs become your thoughts. Your thoughts influence your words. Your words guide your actions. Your actions form your habits. Your habits reflect your values. And ultimately, your values determine your life. Self-awareness holds the key to understanding the process.

Within lies the persistent conflict of our society: our beliefs and values drive our attitude and behavior toward the world. However, society's moral values and ethical rules restrict our actions accordingly. We often choose to conform to the morals and ethics of the society we live in, even if they clash with our values, out of fear of facing repercussions.

Although most people in the world do not murder others, a significant factor contributing to this is the fear of getting caught by the police and the possibility of a life sentence in jail. Of course, there remains a subset of individuals who would never murder under any circumstances. However, the number of those willing to resort to killing would not be zero. Therefore, the presence of laws and a justice system is essential.

Here is the great news about beliefs and values: They are not inscribed into your DNA. Instead, they are learned and have developed and grown within you since your birth. They have evolved based on your environment, experiences, events, and decisions in your life. Today, with elevated self-awareness, you have the power to choose and modify those beliefs and values, replacing them with a new system that empowers and supports your life goals and vision of who you aspire to be.

Your beliefs consist of ideas that you hold to be true. Many of these beliefs, combined with your life circumstances, define your values or what you consider important in life. Your values and beliefs will significantly influence your attitude, affecting how you treat others and yourself and how you approach various situations. Ultimately, these factors shape your behavior or how you act.

Therefore, in the end, your beliefs and values play a direct role in shaping your attitudes and behaviors. By delving deep into your character and understanding these concepts, you can decipher the reasons behind your actions. The best part is that you also have the power to change. If you are dissatisfied with how you behave in a particular context, you can identify the root beliefs and values and shift them to enable different actions.

Your actions, and everything you do, are directly influenced by the values and beliefs that shape your attitudes.

This means that you must first decide what you want to do, which involves creating a vision for yourself or setting up goals to achieve in the future. Next, break down those goals into their constituent parts and assess whether your current set of values and beliefs supports them. If they don't, achieving those goals becomes challenging. This is because your decisions and attitudes will not drive the right behavior necessary to accomplish those goals. Success can only be achieved when your beliefs and values are aligned with your goals.

As I emphasized earlier, beliefs and values are learned; they are not hard-coded into our bodies in any way. We learn to love or hate others, and we learn to love and hate ourselves. All of these are shaped by our life experiences and our very nature as human beings. Some of these beliefs and values have been with you for so long, and you've practiced them, perhaps unconsciously, to the point where they have become habitual and influence your actions and rituals. However, when you take a more thoughtful approach to deciding what your beliefs and values should be, based on your life vision, things change. Your attitude shifts, and consequently, your behavior transforms, leading to different outcomes.

This is powerful stuff because it provides us with an actual lever to change our lives. The problem is that both beliefs and values often carry strong momentum and seem ingrained in our character. We may even feel as though they define who we are. However, once you recognize that this idea is simply not true, you can initiate the process of changing them. It will become apparent that shifting these massive internal frameworks is a long and challenging journey. Nevertheless, it is not impossible. You must acknowledge the truth about your ability to change and embrace the discomfort that comes with the process. To begin, ask yourself: What do I believe about myself? How have these beliefs hindered me from taking action in the past? What do I aspire to become, and what achievements do I desire in the future? To reach those aspirations, how must I alter my beliefs? What holds importance in my life? Have I created a vision for myself? What is my grandest vision for life? What needs to be prioritized so that I can realize that vision?

By engaging in this exercise, you can initiate the process of changing your beliefs and values, shifting them towards a new system that aligns with your goals and vision. It's a challenging journey, filled with hurdles, but at the end of the path awaits a better version of yourself. Go forth and discover that improved version of you, or even better, take action to create that version.

Chapter 9: Become your best self

Now that you have come closer to understanding the journey of self-discovery, it's time to start creating a better self for a brighter future and a brighter society. Many people are good at what they do; some are even elite. But only a selected few are completely unstoppable. Those who are unstoppable exist in their world; they don't compete with anyone but themselves. You never know what they will do, but you will be forced to respond. Although they don't compete with you directly, they inspire you to compete with them.

Let me ask you a question: Are you unstoppable?

Instead of overanalyzing and overthinking, act. Stay attuned to your senses, and trust yourself completely to do what you instinctively feel is right. As Oprah once said: "Every right decision I have ever made has come from my gut. Every wrong decision I've made was the result of me not listening to the greater voice within myself."

Always be prepared, so you have the freedom to act on instinct. Just as the yin-yang symbol possesses a kernel of light in the dark and of dark in the light, creative leaps are grounded in a technical foundation.

Become a master of your craft. While everyone else is relaxing, you're practicing and perfecting. Learn the left-brained rules in and out, so your right brain can have limitless freedom to break the rules and create.

With enhanced consciousness, time will slow down for you. You'll see things in several more frames than others. While they're trying to react to the situation, you'll be able to tweak the situation to your liking.

Don't be motivated solely by money or external. Having nice things is, well, nice. But for you, it has never been about money, prestige, or anything external. Take these things away, and nothing changes for you. You're still going to push your limits and give it your all. If these are given to you, they won't corrupt you as they do for most people.

Never be satisfied. As Tim Grover said, "The drive to close the gap between near-perfect and perfect is the difference between great and unstoppable".

Even after achieving a goal, you're not content. For you, it's not just about the goal itself. It's about the climb pushing yourself to see how far you can go. Does this make you ungrateful? No. You're entirely humbled and grateful for everything in your life. That's precisely why you will never get complacent or lazy.

Always be in control. Unlike most people, who become dependent on substances or other external factors, you maintain control over what you put in your body, how you spend your time, and how long you stay focused in the zone.

Act on instinct, not impulse. Just because you could do something doesn't mean you should. When you do act, it's because you genuinely want to, not because you feel obligated.

Be true to yourself. Even though 70 percent of employees dislike their jobs, and only one in three reports being happy, relentless, and unstoppable people remove everything from their lives that they hate. Have the self-respect and confidence to live life on your terms. When something feels wrong in your life, make an immediate change.

German philosopher Frederick Nietzsche once said, "He who has a why can endure anyhow." Your "why" is the thing that motivates you to get up every morning and work a little harder to become a little better. It's the driving force that keeps you going even on days when all you want to do is pull the covers over your head and hide from the world. Your "why" may change throughout your life, as you experience milestones like getting married, starting a family, or caring for aging parents. Nevertheless, the fundamental questions you need to ask yourself to stay focused and overcome obstacles largely remain the same.

What is your definition of success? Your definition is uniquely yours, and you don't need anyone's approval. There is no need to alter it to fit into some narrow "acceptable" box. However, it's crucial to know what your definition of success is, as it sets your end goal and provides meaning to your efforts. Whether you define success as being able to pay the mortgage and keep the lights on, and that's what motivates you, there is nothing wrong with that.

Once you come up with your definition, dig a little deeper and ask yourself why that is your definition of success. The deeper you dig, the clearer your "why" becomes, and the more motivated you will be to reach it.

Skill and passion are often confused with one another, but they aren't interchangeable. You can be good at what you're doing, and not only lack passion for it but also loathe it entirely. So, ask yourself if you're genuinely passionate about what you're doing, and if not, what are you passionate about? What excites you? What gets you going and motivates you to keep moving forward? Find your "why" and then pursue it with gusto.

You will find more personal and professional fulfillment at the intersection of natural talent, skill, and passion. That is the place where you will find your true motivation and be able to sustain it for the long haul.

If money were no object, what would you do? Money plays a role in motivating all of us to some extent. While it might not be the main driving force, it certainly has an impact. Take a moment to reflect on your current job and ask yourself if you would still be doing it if money were no longer a factor. What would you do in that scenario?

Be realistic, odds are, you aren't going to become a professional athlete or runway model, but take a moment to genuinely contemplate what your dream circumstance would be. If your current situation doesn't align with your aspirations and feels more like a "j-o-b" rather than a fulfilling career, it's time to make a change. Aim for a career that you love and eagerly look forward to, where you can give your all and be your best self. So, how are you going to make that happen? How can you transform your current circumstances (or use them as a starting point) to reach your end goal? It may not be something achievable overnight, but it can serve as the driving force that gets you out of bed in the morning and motivates you to give your best effort now, paving the way to the future you dream of.

One of the biggest "why's" in my life has been making my family proud and my future husband proud. I strive to achieve this both professionally and in my personal life. It's what I'm truly passionate about, and whenever I do make them proud, I feel like I've succeeded.

You will never reach your goals unless you connect with your "why" and periodically reassess to ensure you remain connected to it. But if you are anchored in your "why," the "how" will never be a problem.

Never let off the pressure. "Pressure can bust pipes, but it also can make diamonds," says Tim Grover.

While most people can handle pressure in small doses, they tend to let off the pressure and relax when left to their own devices. Not you. You never release the pressure you put on yourself; instead, you consistently raise it. This approach keeps you alert and active, driving you forward.

Don't be afraid of the consequences of failure. Most people choose to stay close to the ground, where it feels safe. If they fall, it won't hurt that bad. But when you decide to fly high, the fall may be more impactful. And yet, you're OKAY with that. To you, there is no ceiling, and there is no floor; it's all in our heads. If something goes wrong, if you fail, you adjust and keep going.

Never stop learning, this is rule number one for me. Ordinary people seek entertainment, but extraordinary people seek education and continuous learning. When you want to become the best at what you do, you never stop learning. You continually seek improvement and honor your skills and knowledge.

Your unmatched preparation is what gives you power; no one else is willing to pay the price you've paid.

You need to know that success isn't enough, it only increases the pressure. For most people, becoming "successful" is sufficient. However, when you're relentless, success only adds to the pressure to achieve more. Immediately after reaching one goal, you're already focused on your next challenge.

It isn't easy, it requires a significant commitment and unwavering determination each time. But let's face it, sometimes we give up on our goals because we don't follow through on everything we should do. We all do it. So, start today and keep moving forward. Don't be one of those people who never achieve their dreams. Not because you fail (we all make mistakes), but because you should live life with absolutely no regrets. You don't want to go through life knowing you didn't go for it.

I've heard many times from people who have not achieved their goals, and usually, it's not because their goal wasn't a great one; it's because they give up too soon, before reaping the rewards of their efforts.

If this resonated with you, I want you to change your approach and become one of those people who achieve their dreams. I want to share my personal experience and what has worked for me, which I believe can also benefit others. Always strive to be positive and non-judgmental. I have always believed that everything starts with a positive mindset. While it's okay to not be okay sometimes, having a mindset built on uplifting statements makes you resilient and helps you quickly get back on your feet. What you set your mind to is where you will put action. You must believe in yourself and stay positive as much as you can. Some of the best ways to do this are to surround yourself with positive, inspiring people, journal your progress, and start each day reading an inspirational article or listening to something positive and motivational.

Be persistent. When you are striving to achieve a significant goal, there will be people who say NO to what you want and need. I have experienced this, and you will too. Strong, successful people do not give up easily. While you don't want to push too hard on people, sometimes it only takes a 15 percent shift in your strategy. And sometimes, it's that very next person who will say YES. So, keep moving forward with your goals. Always believe that today is going to be your day.

Having amazing patience is crucial when pursuing your biggest goals. We all want to achieve our goals quickly, to reap the fruits of our labor immediately. However, sometimes the timing isn't right for our aspirations. As Beverly Sills said: "There are no shortcuts to any place worth going." Embrace a mindset that believes the wait will be worthwhile. Take massive action on anything you can, but also remember that great things take time. Your dreams are undoubtedly worth the wait.

Throughout our lives, there will be people and situations that try to throw us off our path to success. Some will tell you that you can't do it, and challenges along the way may tempt you to quit. Resilience is a crucial quality to have in order to succeed. If you find yourself doubting at times, one of the best things you can do is hire a mentor or coach to help you positively push through when needed. Alone, you can accomplish a lot, but with the right support system, you'll find that you can achieve so much more.

As Og Mandino said: "Always take the attitude of a student. Never be too big to ask questions, never know too much to learn something new." You must always be willing to learn and grow

My Own Identity: An Introduction to Self-Discovery

throughout life because it will lead you to great success. Keep an open mind to the awesome possibilities and opportunities out there. Surround yourself with intelligent individuals from whom you can learn and grow. Being around people who have already walked the path you're on will expose you to incredible strategies for achieving success.

You deserve to achieve your goals and dreams. If you truly want it, you have to go for it, but remember that taking the right steps is essential for success. Stay positive, be persistent yet patient, develop resilience, and always be adaptable.

Success can become a catalyst for failure. For most people, handling success, authority, or privilege becomes a challenge—it can destroy them and make them lazy. When they achieve their goals, they stop doing the very things that got them there. The external noise becomes too intense. But for you, no external noise can push harder than your internal pressure. It's not just about this achievement, but the one after, and the one after, and the one after that. There is no destination; keep going until you're finished. And when you do screw up, you completely own it.

"Implementing extreme ownership requires checking your ego and operating with a high degree of humility. Admitting mistakes, taking ownership, and developing a plan to overcome challenges are integral to any successful team." Sya Jocko Willink in his book *Extreme Ownership: How U.S. Navy SEALs Lead and Win.*

No blame. No deception or illusion. Just the cold, hard truth. When you mess up, you own it. And as the leader, you own it when your team fails. Only with extreme ownership can you have complete freedom and control.

If I always took 100 percent responsibility for everything I experienced, completely owning all of my choices and all the ways I respond to whatever, happened to me, I held the power. Everything was up to me. I was responsible for everything I did, didn't do, or how I responded to what was done to me.

I know many of you think that you take responsibility for your life. I've yet to ask anybody who doesn't say: "Of course, I take responsibility for my life." But when you look at how most people operate in the world, there's a lot of finger-pointing, victimhood, blaming, and expecting someone else or the government to solve their problems. If you've ever blamed traffic for being late or decided you are in a bad mood because of something your kid, spouse, or co-worker did, you're not taking 100 percent personal responsibility. Did you arrive late because the printer was busy? Maybe you shouldn't have waited until the last minute. Did a co-worker mess up the presentation? Shouldn't you have double-checked it yourself before delivering it? Not getting along with your unreasonable child? There are countless fantastic books and classes to help you learn how to deal with it.

You alone are responsible for what you do, don't do, or how you respond to what's done to you. This empowering mindset revolutionized my life. Luck, circumstances, or the right situation didn't matter. If it was to be, it was up to me. I was free to fly. No matter who was elected president, how badly the economy tanked, or what anybody said, did, or didn't do, I was still 100 percent in control of myself. By choosing to be officially liberated from past, present, and future victimhood, I hit the jackpot. I had the unlimited power to control my destiny in some way or another.

Let your work speak for itself. Well done is well said. Talking is shallow. Anyone can do it. It's easily replicated. It's low value. Conversely, deep work is rare. It's done by people who are focused and working while everyone else is talking. Deep work is so good it can't be ignored. It doesn't need words. It speaks for itself.

Always work on your mental strength. "Mental resilience is arguably the most critical trait of any human being, and it should be nurtured continually. Left to my own devices, I am always looking for ways to become more and more psychologically impregnable. When uncomfortable, my instinct is not to avoid the discomfort but to become at peace with it. My instinct is always to seek out challenges as opposed to avoiding them." – Josh Waitzkin.

The better you can be under pressure, the further you'll go than anyone else, because they'll crumble under pressure. The best training you will ever do is mental training. Wherever your mind goes, your body follows. Wherever your thoughts go, your life follows.

Chapter 10: Reaching your greatest potential

Throughout my hardest time, I realized that focusing on my strengths and ignoring my weaknesses had serious limitations. If I wanted to emerge from that painful period stronger than before, I needed to pay close attention to the bad habits that held me back. Letting myself feel like a victim, complaining about my circumstances, and distracting myself from the pain might help me feel better in the short term, but eventually would cause more problems over the long term.

My hardships taught me that it only takes one or two bad habits, no matter how minor they might seem, to stall progress.

Reaching your greatest potential doesn't require you to work harder by adding desirable habits to your already busy life. Instead, you can work smarter by eliminating the routines that erode effectiveness and siphon off mental strength.

Have you ever seen a cartoon with a snowball perched on top of a hill? You know what happens: It starts rolling, slowly at first, and then faster and faster, growing with each revolution, flattening all in its path or gobbling up bystanders, their arms and legs sticking out at impossible angles. My grandfather was a physician; he used this image a lot when I was little to explain how a simple push can make a big difference.

It is basic physics that describes two kinds of energy at play in this situation: potential and kinetic energy. Potential energy refers to the energy that an object could have as it sits at the top of the hill. Because of forces like gravity, the snowball has the potential to move down the hill.

As the snowball rolls, it exerts kinetic energy. This is the energy of motion. All it takes is a little push, and the object starts rolling. There may be resistance along the way, but usually, the momentum is enough to keep it moving.

Do you see where I'm going with this? I meet people all the time who are like that snowball at the top of the hill. They are filled with extraordinary potential, but all too often, they just sit there. They won't give themselves that little push to get started, and all of that potential energy goes to waste.

Every person has the seed of potential inside, but few people ever fully grow it. When it comes to meeting and conquering the negativity in your life, here is a key question: What can you do, starting today, that will make a difference?

What can you do when everything has gone wrong? What can you do if you've run out of money? What can you do when you don't feel well? What can you do when it's all gone sour? What can you do?

Let me give you the broad answer first...

You can do the most remarkable things, no matter what happens. People can do incredible things, unbelievable things, despite the most impossible or disastrous circumstances.

Why can humans do remarkable things? Because they are remarkable. Humans are distinct from any other creation. When a dog starts with weeds, he ends up with weeds. The reason is that he's a dog. However, that is not true for human beings. Humans can transform weeds into gardens.

If something isn't sufficient, change it. If something doesn't suit you, change it. We possess the capacity to change. Humans can turn nothing into something, pennies into fortune, and disaster into success. The reason we can achieve such remarkable feats is that we are remarkable ourselves. Try reaching down inside of yourself, and you will uncover some remarkable human gifts. We are there, waiting to be discovered and utilized.

With those gifts, you can change anything for yourself that you wish to alter. I challenge you to embrace change because you have the power to transform. If you're dissatisfied with the current situation, change it. If something falls short, change it. If something fails to bring you joy, change it. You don't have to accept things as they are; you have the freedom to change! Remember, you're not a tree; you're not rooted in place. You can be different from who you were just today.

If there is one thing worth getting excited about, you can motivate yourself to take necessary actions, achieve desired results, and turn adversity into success. And that's truly remarkable.

Everyone possesses this potential within; all we need to do is look inside ourselves. However, four basic mistakes that tend to hinder our progress. Let's explore these mistakes in detail so that we can unleash our personal momentum.

Mistake number 1: Waste time feeling sorry for ourselves. It's futile to wallow in our problems, exaggerate our misfortunes, and keep score of how many hardships we've endured. Whether we're struggling to pay our bills or experiencing serious health problems, throwing a pity party only worsens the situation. Self-pity keeps us fixated on the problem and prevents us from developing a solution. Hardship and sorrow are inevitable, but feeling sorry for yourself is a choice. Even when you can't solve the problem, you can choose to control your attitude. Find three things to be grateful for every day to keep self-pity at bay.

Mistake number 2: Giving away the power. Feeling like a victim and being mentally strong are mutually exclusive; they cannot coexist. If your thoughts lead you into a victim mindset, such as saying, "My mom drives me crazy" or "My friend makes me feel bad about myself," you unwittingly grant others power over you. The truth is that no one has control over the way you think, feel, or behave except for you.

Changing your daily vocabulary is one way to recognize that the choices you make are yours. Instead of saying, "I have to work later today," edit that sentiment to "I'm choosing to stay late."

There may be consequences if you don't work late, but it remains your choice. Empowering yourself is an essential component of creating the kind of life you want.

Mistake number 3: Shying away from change. If you constantly worry that change will make things worse, you'll end up staying stuck in your old ways and inadvertently making things worse. The world is constantly evolving, and your success depends on your ability to adapt. The more you practice tolerating distress from various sources, such as taking a new job or leaving an unhealthy relationship, the more confident you'll become in your ability to adapt and create positive change in yourself.

Mistake number 4: Squandering energy on things we don't control. Complaining, worrying, and wishful thinking don't solve problems; they only waste your energy. But, if you invest that same energy in the things you can control, you'll be much better prepared for whatever life throws your way.

Pay attention to the times when you're tempted to worry about things you can't control, such as the weather, the choices other people make, or how your competitor behaves. Redirect this energy towards something more productive, like completing a project at work or home, or helping a friend with hers. Accept situations that are beyond your control and focus on influencing, rather than controlling, people around you.

Mistake number 5: Worrying about pleasing everyone. Whether we are anxious that our mother will criticize our latest endeavor or attending an event we would rather skip to avoid a guilt trip, trying to make other people happy drains our mental strength and causes us to lose sight of our goals.

Making choices that disappoint or upset others takes courage, but living an authentic life requires you to act according to your values.

Mistake number 6: Fearing to take risks. When something appears scary, you might not shy away from taking the risk, even if it's a small one. Conversely, if you're excited about a new opportunity, you may overlook a significant risk and charge ahead. Emotions can cloud your judgment and interfere with your ability to accurately assess risk. You can't become extraordinary without taking chances, but the success of the outcome depends on your ability to assess and manage the risks effectively.

Acknowledge how you're feeling about a certain risk and recognize how your emotions influence your thoughts. Create a list of the pros and cons of taking the risk to help you make a decision based on a balance of emotion and logic.

Mistake number 7: Dwelling on the past. Learning from the past helps you build mental strength, but ruminating is harmful. Constantly questioning your past choices or romanticizing about the good old days prevents you from both enjoying the present and making the future as good as it can be. Reflecting on the past is beneficial at times, especially to acknowledge how far you've come. However, the most important aspect is to make peace with the past. This process might involve forgiving someone who hurt you, and at other times, moving forward means letting go of things that no longer serve you well, most importantly, letting go of regret. Rather than reliving your past, work through the painful emotions that keep you stuck.

Mistake number 8: Repeating their mistakes. Whether you felt embarrassed when you gave the wrong answer in class or were scolded for messing up, you may have learned from a young age that mistakes are bad. Consequently, you might hide or excuse your mistakes to avoid associating yourself with them, but doing so will prevent you from learning from them.

Whether you regained the weight you worked hard to lose or forgot an important deadline, view each misstep as an opportunity for growth. Set aside your pride and humbly evaluate why you made the mistake. Use that knowledge to move forward, improving yourself from before.

Mistake number 9: Resenting other people's successes. Watching a friend receive a promotion, hearing another friend's latest achievement, or seeing a family member buy a car you can't afford can stir up feelings of envy. However, jealousy shifts the focus from your efforts and interferes with your ability to reach your goals.

Write down your definition of success. When you're secure in that definition, you'll stop resenting others for attaining their goals, and you'll stay committed to reaching yours. Recognize that when other people achieve their goals, it doesn't diminish your accomplishments. What God has for you is uniquely yours. If He blesses your neighbor, it means God is present in the neighborhood, and you might be next.

Mistake number 10: Giving up after the first failure. Some people avoid failure at all costs because it unravels their sense of self-worth. Not trying at all or giving up after your first attempt will prevent you from reaching your potential. Almost every story of a wildly successful person starts with tales of repeated failure.

Face your fear of defeat head-on by stretching yourself to your limits. Even when you feel embarrassed, rejected, or ashamed, hold your head high and refuse to let lack of success define you as a person. Focus on improving your skills and be willing to try again after you fail.

Mistake number 11: Fear of alone time. Solitude can sometimes feel unproductive. For some people, the thought of being alone with their thoughts is downright scary. As a result, most people avoid silence by filling their days with a flurry of activity and background noise.

However, alone time is an essential component of building your mental strength. Carve out at least 10 minutes each day to gather your thoughts without the distractions of the world. Use the time to reflect on your progress and create goals for the future.

Mistake number 12: Feeling the world owes you something. We often like to think that if we put in enough hard work or tough it out through bad times, then we deserve success. However, waiting for the world to give you what you think you're owed isn't a productive life strategy.

Take notice of times when you feel as though you deserve something better. Intentionally focus on all that you have to give rather than what you think you deserve. Regardless of whether you think you've been dealt a fair hand in life, you have gifts to share with others.

Mistake number 13: Expecting immediate results. Self-growth develops slowly. Whether you're trying to shed your procrastination tendencies or improve your marriage, expecting instant results will lead to disappointment. Think of your efforts as a marathon, not a spring. View bumps in the road as minor setbacks rather than total roadblocks.

You'll need all the mental strength you can muster at some point in your life, whether it's coping with the loss of a loved one, facing financial hardships, or dealing with a major health problem. Mental strength will give you the resilience to push through these challenges.

And the great news is that everyone can strengthen their mental muscle. Practice being your mental strength coach. Pay attention to areas in which you're doing well and identify areas that need improvement. Create opportunities for growth and challenge yourself to become a little better today than you were yesterday.
No matter what innate talents you were born with, what family you were born into, the money you have made or lost, or the times of difficulty or lucky breaks, nothing will get you to where you want to be better than understanding your full potential.

It's the decisive factor in every successful story. Whether it's the popular "Poor man gets lucky" tale or the "How I changed the world with my bare hands" narrative, one important factor remains— the people who succeed are those who learn how to tap into something innate inside them and live and breathe their dreams.

Each one of us has potential lying innate inside of us. The brilliant part is each one of us has a potential that is uniquely ours. A mad mix of our genetics, environment, the way our body has been designed, and the talents we were born with. Each one of us has something different, gifts to impart to this world.

Of course, the first step is discovering just what that is. For some, this is an instinctive process, often helped by a watchful parent or teacher who spotted something in us from an early age and called it into being.

For others, it's a struggle to identify their true potential. That can be for a range of reasons. As young children, we often have instinctive ideas of what we want to do. However, these aspirations can be torn from us or pushed down by parental disapproval or expectations that don't align with our natural talents. For instance, I may have been created as a creative person who loves to put words and phrases together, but I come from a long line of accountants and farmers, creating an expectation that I should be in a similar field. Luckily for me, my family was open-minded and supportive, allowing me to choose the field and life that I see myself in.

The environment can also play a part. Often, we learn about what we are good at by trying new things. If you lived in an area with limited opportunities, as I did, or didn't have the financial means to pay for classes or travel, you may not have had the chance to experience the things you are naturally good at.

Sometimes our ambition, mixed with false beliefs can get in the way.

The first step to discovering your potential is to realize that no matter your physical, financial, or environmental limitations, you, I, and the vast majority of humanity share one very important asset in common: Our Mind.

Our mind can work with us and for us to help us reach our goals. Once we unlock the keys our mind holds, we have the opportunity to do the following:
- Learn to override the fears of failure and not being good enough. Let go of social phobias and the hold of limiting beliefs.
- Discover the talents and gifts we were given and how we can develop them.
- Learn how to spot new opportunities for personal growth and learn new skills.
- Set goals you had always thought were the goals of dreamers and then achieve those goals.
- Develop a strong sense of purpose and direction. Understand the value of your life in this world and the difference your new life can make.
- Become someone who loves to face challenges and then meets and overcomes them. Discover the fun in conquering the mountains of challenges in your own life, no longer accepting the status quo as an acceptable standard.
- Learn the benefits of a balanced life where your physical, emotional, spiritual, and financial health live in harmony with each other, leading to a sense of fulfillment and satisfaction with your life.

By investing time to unlock your potential, you have the opportunity to discover all that you were created to be. Part of that process is identifying what your purpose is. To do that, you need to first look at what makes you feel passionate. A life lived with passion is a life lived fully.

For some, a life lived passionately is second nature. They seem to know the direction they should go in almost from birth, and everything always seems to fall into place for them. They are like a cat falling from a height— no matter what, they always seem to land on their feet.

However, for many people, it takes a sharp change, a crystal clear moment, or a long journey of learning to find that same direction. I am one of these people, and I know it can be learned and discovered by spending some time investigating your history.

If you want to succeed in life, you must first find your passion, then harness it and use it to focus your dreams and vision. The more you follow the path your passion leads you, the more you achieve the goals you desire, and your life starts to fall into place.

A person without passion cannot change, as they have no motivation to do so. While not everything we do is directly related to our passion, if we are assured of our passion, we approach all those extra tasks more gladly, knowing that passion will drive us through the bits we find hard and less enjoyable.

That is one of the secrets of living a life where you meet your full potential.

As we are all different, we will all need different paths to help us find our passion and purpose. If you've struggled to find the direction you need to fulfill your destiny, if you've always felt you were made for something but are a little unsure what it was, then try some of the following ideas that helped me explore my purpose and may help you discover yours.

Everyone has a purpose, and there is potential in each of us. It's just a matter of exploring and investigating a little to discover it.

What terrifies you? It's an interesting concept, but what you don't like or what you fear may be the very thing pointing to your destiny. It's like the concept of yin and yang; there are two sides to each coin. The fear may originate from blocking off an early passion that you were unaware of. Write a list of your fears and the negative feelings that comes from them. Then look at that list and see if there is an opposite charge to the fear. For example, if you are terrified of public speaking but love to share your ideas, then you may be well suited to expressing yourself through the written word.

When are you scared of failing? Those things that are important to us hold a great deal of weight in how we see ourselves and our success. If you are scared of failing at something, you'll often avoid it at all costs. But those things we are scared to fail at are often the very things we most want to do. Explore the times you've said no to something or avoided something you've been scared of, showing yourself to not be good at.

Who energizes you? If you've only got people around you who tear or wear you down, and you struggle with feeling good about yourself when you are around them, then you need to change the dynamic. What sort of people inspire you? What sort of people make you want to grab life and live it completely, who adds a little light to everything? The people we are attracted to, and those we want to spend time with, reflect not only where we are but where we want to be. Align yourself with people living a full life, and their enthusiasm rubs off and affects your passion. Go for people you respect and work under or alongside them — serving them. That is the very best way to learn. If you can't find anyone like that around you, devour books about people you admire and learn by proxy.

When will you get there? It can be incredibly frustrating when you can see where you want to end up (and how many of us have the dream of a house, traveling around the world). However, each journey starts with one small step in front of the other. The end destination isn't the only thing you need; you need to break it right down into manageable chunks. You may start with a small passion for something really simple that you don't think much of, and then it explodes and evolves into something else entirely. Enjoy that process, and trust it. The lessons we learn along the way as we explore our purpose are never waster.

If you are naturally visionary, having to wait it out sometimes can be incredibly frustrating. However, learning to temper your impatience and lay it aside helps you get there faster. Remembering there is a season for everything you do helps.

Who are you now? Before you start to move forward, you need to first make peace with the person you are today, right here and right now. The person you are today is the person you started to become five or ten years ago. We are all a product of our past and the place we are in today, with all our foibles and limitations. If you've got a few pounds to lose or spend money like it's going out of fashion. If you're in a dead-end job because you've never really used that initiative lying innate in all of us, or you are in a relationship that is more about comfort than seeing each other move towards each other's purpose, the only person who put there is you.

Love yourself now; accept yourself now and where you have been, and then move on. Our purpose can begin from any circumstance. No matter what has gone before, we have the choice to change our life now, today.

One person in themselves can be hugely effective. Dream big and don't underestimate your ability to get there— many people have dreamed up a purpose that, on paper looked impossible but was not only achieved but surpassed. Breathe life into those big visions.

What will I do? Make a list of all the dreams and thoughts you've had— all the things you want to do in your life. Once it's down on paper, make a plan of action to follow. Sometimes the first step is to consolidate, regroup, and spend some time learning or preparing. This is an excellent time to give your time to work under people who are working towards a similar purpose and to learn alongside them.

Don't worry if the times get a little rough sometimes. See, the difficult times are periods of growth, where you are learning the next important lessons to succeed. There is a well-known Chinese proverb that says: "When things are going good, the business grows; when things are going bad, you grow." No experience is ever wasted as long as you grasp any circumstance as an opportunity to grow. For example, right now I am in a situation where I feel like nothing works out in my favor. It is a hard time emotionally because of some failed experience, and look at me now, I am using this energy to write, to learn from experience, and to share it with the world, hoping that it will help others too. I am channeling this energy or resentment into powerful energy to grow. It is not easy, but it is worth the time.

Who cares what other people do? Your unique passion is never going to be the same as someone else's. Sure, there will be elements the same, but the majority of your purpose is a custom fit for you. Just as others can't mass-produce your purpose for themselves, you can't look at someone else's purpose and compare your own to it in a negative light. You can only be yourself and bring your talents and skills to your purpose. No one will do it quite like you. And that is ok!

When we start to look at how others fulfill a similar vision, we can start to make negative judgments about ourselves. Of course, looking and learning positively way is a clever way to save a few big mistakes along the way. But when you allow fear to creep into your comparison times, your purpose suffers.

When will you get there? Your purpose is likely to change and evolve as you do. Once you begin to grasp the sense of fun and excitement that comes from exploring your purpose, you will want it to change and evolve with you. Get ready to embark on a lifelong journey of discovering your purpose. To begin with, your goals may be small. We can only conceive in our heads that which we truly believe we can achieve. If you've ever had a big dream and focused on it, you might find your mind often putting up blocks or reasons why that dream won't happen for you. The key is to constantly try to stretch the dream we have for our purpose.

That means we may need to rework our purpose every five to ten years. What motivates you in your twenties may not give you the same rush in your thirties. Keep a check on yourself and what you want to be living in the now— not what you wanted five years ago. If you are reading this as a teen or young person, use your youth to your best advantage. The time we have as a single person, with no huge amounts of responsibilities, including paying all those boring bills and having a partner, is the very best time to use our time well and experience as much of life as we can. Spend this time not only studying but also learning skills in leadership, organization, and people skills through voluntary work, hobbies, and general life.

No matter your age, become someone who says "yes" to life, as then you open yourself up to opportunities. As you begin to say yes, you start to see new ways to achieve your purpose that you may have thought were unlikely before. Never say you are too busy to get there. As the saying goes: "If you want something done, give it to a busy person." A person who is busy in life, not just busy trying to wearily make it to the next bedtime, actually has the time to do the things they want to do. We all have choices in how we spend our time. Use it well and wisely.

How did I get here? Being thankful every day for where you are now, and where you are going, keeps your thoughts on track. If you can't be thankful for any aspect of your life, then it is likely that you are living a life that is not consistent with the purpose you were designed for. And if you have lost that ability to be thankful, you need to start to create it to give yourself the strength to move out of that negative situation.

Start the day with thankfulness. Before you get up in the morning, say some thank you. If you have faith, this is like praying. However, the concept works regardless; it's just acknowledging the things in your life you love or care about. It may be people, situations, or possessions.

At the end of the day, just before bed, repeat the exercise. This way, you start and end the day on a positive note. It doesn't take a lot of time, and it's a good way to create a circle of thankfulness to set up and end your day on.

Chapter 11: Have clear goals

"While a fixation on results is certainly unhealthy, short-term goals can be useful developmental tools if they are balanced within a nurturing long-term philosophy."
– Josh Waitzkin

According to loads of psychological research, the most motivating goals are clearly defined and time-bound. Your goals can either be focused on your behaviors or on the outcomes you're seeking.

For most people, behaviorally-focused goals are the better and more motivating option. But when you crave the results so much that the work becomes irrelevant, your aim should be directed straight at the outcomes you want. However, results-focused goals are better when short-term and grounded in your long-term vision and philosophy. When your "why" is strong enough, the "how" will take care of itself.

Goal setting is a fantastic skill to develop and a way to design your future. A life best lived is a life by design, not by accident, and not just by walking through the day careening from wall to wall, merely managing to survive. If you can start giving your life dimensions, design, color, objectives, and purpose, the results can be staggering.

Goal setting gives you the chance to experience the power of your imagination. Think about it. Imagination builds cities. Imagination conquers disease. Imagination develops careers. Imagination sets up relationships. Imagination is where all tangible and intangible values begin. So what you've got to learn to do is use this powerful resource.

Tapping this resource of imagination for goal setting involves thinking about your future, pondering tomorrow or the rest of the day, and considering the rest of the year or five years, or even ten years. You can use your imagination to start prospecting for the future, exploring what could be possible for you.

Learning to set goals can transform your life forever. There is power in reaching out into the future, designing something to the best of your ability, refining it as you go, and even tearing it up periodically if you want to, to set a whole new list. It's your life. It's your future.

The major reason for setting a goal is the impact it has on what you do to accomplish it. This will always hold far greater value than what you get. That is why goals are so powerful. They are woven into the fabric that makes up our lives.

Goal setting is powerful because it provides focus, shapes our dreams, and gives us the ability to home in on the exact actions we need to take to achieve everything in life we desire. Goals cause us to stretch and grow in ways we never have before. To reach our goals, we must become better; we must change and grow.

As I study that powerful goal, I have identified three components:
1. It must be inspiring.
2. It must be believable.
3. It must be goals you can act on.

Life is designed in such a way that we look long term and live short term. We dream for the future and live in the present. Unfortunately, the present can present many hard obstacles. Fortunately, the more powerful our goals are— because they are inspiring and believable— the more we will be able to act on them in the short term and guarantee that they will come to pass.

So, what are the key aspects to learn and remember when studying and writing our goals?

First of all, reflection and evaluation. The only way we can reasonably decide what we want in the future and how we will get there is to first know where we are right now and what our current level of satisfaction is. With our focus on goal setting, the first order of business for each of us is to set aside some serious time for evaluation and reflection.

Top-level athletes, successful business people, and achievers in all fields all set goals. Setting goals gives you long-term vision and short-term motivation. It focuses on your acquisition of knowledge and helps you to organize your time and resources so that you can make the most of your life.

By setting sharp, clearly defined goals, you can measure and take pride in the achievement of those goals, and you'll see forward progress in what might previously have seemed like a long, pointless grind. You will also raise your self-confidence as you recognize your ability and competence in achieving the goals that you've set.

You set your goals on several levels. First, you create your "big picture" of what you want to do with your life (or over, say, the next 10 years) and identify the large-scale goals that you want to achieve. Then, you break these down into smaller and smaller targets that you must hit to reach your lifetime goals. Finally, once you have your plan, you start working on it to achieve these goals.

This is why we start the process of setting goals by looking at our lifetime goals. Then, we work down to the things that we can do in, say, the next five years, next year, next month, next week, and today, to start moving toward them. One step at a time.

Before you set a goal, take a closer look at what you're trying to achieve and ask yourself the following questions: Is this goal something you truly want? Is it important enough to invest hours of time and effort into it?

If you are not willing to put in the time, it may not be worth pursuing. If you create a long list of goals to pursue all at the same time, you may have a difficult time achieving any of them. Instead, use the questions above to determine which goals matter the most to you right now, and then focus on those few.

After identifying what you desire, make sure your goals align with the SMART criteria:

- Specific
- Measurable
- Attainable
- Realistic
- Time-bound

The most important part of SMART goal setting is to make your goal specific so you can track your process and know whether you met the goal. The most specific you can be with your goal, the higher the chance you'll complete it.

First, I want you to think of a moment in your lifetime when you accomplished something— big or small. This moment should be a time when you felt at your best. Maybe it was work-related or personal achievement? What I want you to focus on first is how you felt at that exact moment. Feel free to write these emotions down on a piece of paper or in your notes on your phone.

My moment would have to be the first time I hosted a conference in Los Angeles. It was a group of about 50 or 60 people. As we began to wrap up the one-hour program, I asked for thoughts and takeaways from the day. The comments and conversations we had overwhelmed me with emotions—good emotions. I felt accomplished, helpful, proud, humble, motivated, and joyful. Most of all, I overcame the fear of public speaking.

Now, let's go back to your moment and think about how you felt. What made that moment possible? How did you get to that exact moment in your life?

My moment took months of practice and patience. I had already spent a whole year working with the organization, but this one was different. I had to allow myself to be vulnerable and open-minded. I practiced in front of the mirror, learned every expression, imagined how everything would be set up, and disciplined myself to practice more. Practice makes a person better.

Lastly, what are your goals now? What are you working towards? Maybe you want to work on a new project or start a new hobby. Perhaps it is to save up a certain amount of money or to make yourself workout three times a week? Whatever your goal may be, it is achievable.

For instance, my goal at this stage was to finish my book, and now you are reading it, which means any goal can be achievable if you really want this to happen. I love spending time alone and writing. My imagination can take me from one place to another and make me think about many other things— life, people, surroundings, and so on.

Hopefully, I will have a role that helps me grow professionally and personally while inspiring others to do the same. I, of course, set little goals along the way, such as setting aside time to work out throughout the week, eating healthier, and listening to new audiobooks at least once a week. No goal is too big or too small. You just have to want it bad enough.

No goal is too outrageous or impossible to reach. If you rewind with me a little, you'll see why. You have set goals for yourself, and you can make them happen because you have done it before. Think back to how you got to your moment— the moment that made you feel your best. Maybe it took patience, endurance, or discipline; maybe you had the support of family and friends. With all the skills and resources it took to achieve those big current goals, you will be overwhelmed with feelings like before. You'll have a sense of pride, achievement, and happiness. You are your biggest resource. Dig deep to find your passions, skills, and talents and use them. Make your goals a reality.

The process of setting goals makes you succeed faster and more efficiently. It can fuel your ambition and help you achieve tangible results. A goal-setting process will help you determine how to set goals that are specific, timely, and realistic.

Putting your goals, process, and progress on paper is extremely powerful. I find that it gives me a different perspective on my own decisions. It's almost as if the distance that the journal affords me from my brain and mind helps me be more objective.

It's also interesting to see, when you read back in your journal, how much you've grown and how your thought processes have changed.

Writing down your achievements is wonderful; it's motivating and inspiring.

When setting the direction to success, you must make good choices about the path you are going to choose. The wrong path will lead you somewhere that takes you off track from your goals. This path can lead to partying too much, getting lazy, and neglecting your chores. You must stay on top and not fall behind.

Drive plays a big part in setting goals. Without the drive, you lose sight of the nice things that can be achieved with hard work, or better said, with smart work. The drive also motivates you to do the things that you don't want to do but have to do—things like writing papers, studying, chores, and many others. The drive to achieve your goals will help you through these tough times. During challenging moments, think about all those goals you are trying to achieve and how nice it will be when you reach them.

Finding a career that will provide for you can be very difficult if you do not follow the path to reach your goals. This is another reason to stay on track. Without your education, going into the workforce and finding a good job that will provide for you and your family can be very hard. Most jobs require a school degree and sometimes certifications that require many hours of work. Without degrees and certifications, advancement in a job is sometimes impossible for some. Without advancement in a career, it is very hard to reach your goals of making that big salary and having all of the enjoyable things in life.

Achieving any goal requires self-discipline. It involves a conscious awareness of our actions and the ability to overcome some of the bad habits that might be holding us back. Instilling self-discipline into our lives is not an easy task. It requires steady attention to our actions and determination to achieve something big. To achieve your goal in life, you need to deeply desire the goal that you want. Weak desires bring weak results. You need to have a strong desire and decide what you want. Start to think about what these goals mean to you. Take time to think about why you are setting the goal you have chosen.

Once you set your goal, you need to start getting more specific. It moves from a dream into reality. Make a plan; it must move from your mind to a piece of paper. Write down the things you need to do: What do you want to achieve? What will be your life when you achieve your goal? Things that it needs to be done. Things that you want to learn more about your goal. Qualities that you admire in others. Improve the qualities you have. Habits that you want to stop and habits you want to improve.

The ideas and activities in this chapter help your mind lock in the purpose you are heading to. It helps you place your goals inside your subconscious, and then the process becomes a lot easier.

The ability to harness your mind and control your thought processes is one that successful people throughout the ages have used. It's the common denominator of all successful people, whether they are busy owners or world-class athletes.

Research into the ability to drive past our own limiting beliefs has shown that if we get the mind on track, the rest will follow.

Techniques such as using mantras and positive thinking have been able to bring healing to the body, pushing back the effects of even terminal illnesses such as cancer.

Many people believe that when we begin to take control of our minds and focus on our goals, we affect the environment we live in. Exciting things begin to happen, with doors that seemed so heavily wedged shut opening, or new opportunities springing out of nowhere. These are situations that begin to work in your favor once you get your focus right.

Even at the very worst, a more positive attitude is likely to help you become more open to opportunities and be more on the lookout for new ideas and opening doors.

Turn your life into the life you want by discovering the purpose you were born to live and then change the way you think of yourself, living that life to get there. Remember the place you are now is the place you got to by the thoughts you've already had—even if it was not a conscious decision.

Start to take your future place in this world into both your conscious and subconscious mind, learning to turn around and move ahead to reach your purpose. It won't take long to enjoy the fruits of your endeavors.

Chapter 12: Have faith in your capabilities

Believing in yourself means having faith in your capabilities. It means believing that you "CAN" do something, that it is within your ability. When you believe in yourself, you can overcome self-doubt and have the confidence to take action and get things done.

In business and your personal life, self-confidence is a prerequisite for taking massive action. You need to believe in yourself to take the leap into entrepreneurship or pursue any other aspiration. This is the lynchpin of exceptional leadership because self-confidence enables you to manage and inspire others with assurance and direction.

When you think of it this way, answering the question, "Why is it important to believe in yourself?" is easy: Learning how to believe in yourself is critical to creating the life you desire. Many of us are aware of this, but during challenging times, we tend to doubt our abilities and succumb to fears. Self-belief requires a holistic strategy. You must take control of your thoughts and feelings to reach your peak state. It also entails building up confidence in your abilities and embracing the uniqueness of your personality, perspective, and experiences of who you are.

This is where personal power is built: by claiming agency to overcome challenges in your life. Believing isn't about experiencing uninterrupted success; it's about being able to bounce back from failure quickly. To do that, you must change your perspective on failure. Tony Robbins has said: "I've come to believe that all my past failures and frustrations were laying the foundation for the understandings that have created the new level of living I now enjoy." This is his top tip for believing in yourself: See failures as opportunities, not obstacles. Learn from them, get up, and pursue your goals.

Asking how to believe in yourself opens the door to a deeper question: What are the beliefs that are causing these emotions in the first place? Negative emotions, life, self-doubts, and anxiety are deeply connected to the opinions we have of ourselves based on our experiences. They're your brain signaling that it's time to examine these limiting beliefs and replace them with empowering ones. However, that can be easier said than done. One way to get started is to focus on your self-talk.

Self-love is the foundation of self-belief. If you don't love yourself, how can you ever learn to have faith in yourself? And if you don't know yourself, how can you ever truly love yourself? To master the art of self-confidence, first, master the arts of self-awareness and self-love. Determine your values as we discussed in Chapter 8. Embrace your strengths and weaknesses equally. That doesn't mean you can't work on those weaknesses. It's about appreciating who you are and what makes you different from everyone else on the planet. When you start questioning your self-belief, remember to love yourself first.

To tap into your power, you need to adopt new routines. Consider building a meditation practice, as mindfulness meditation is shown to reduce anxiety and help you focus on your core competencies. Visualization is a technique used by many because it works. You can even try incantations, a powerful way to use your body and voice to set intentions. Alternatively, start the day with priming, an exercise routine. By incorporating techniques for believing in yourself into your morning routine, you can set the tone for a day filled with confidence.

Learning how to believe in yourself is like running a race set on an uphill course. You'll need fuel for the journey. To fuel self-belief, surround yourself with people who inspire and support you; this is the law of attraction. Whatever you want to achieve in your life, find people who will elevate you, not bring you down. You can do this by finding a mentor or joining a like-minded group of people— different from your group of friends or your family. When you tap into the power of proximity, you'll gain a trusted advisor who can not only support you but also challenge you to do better.

The law of attraction isn't just about who you associate with; it's also about how you feed your mind: what you read and watch daily. Make a point to seek advice from others who have achieved your goals, even if they are not your method or coach. Watch documentaries about people who have accomplished great things in life. Learn about new topics that will help you reach your goals, such as finance or overcoming fears, building confidence, and delivering presentations. By doing so, you'll condition your brain to believe in yourself because it will recognize that you have the skills needed to succeed. Sometimes, you don't need external support to believe in yourself. If you're feeling discouraged, shift your focus. Instead of dwelling on failures, weaknesses, or things beyond your control, recall moments in your past when you were successful at a similar task or when your strengths shone through. Reflect on obstacles you faced and overcame with grace and courage. Focus on all the things you have to be grateful for, rather than fixating on what you lack. By concentrating on the positive, you can transform your mindset from one of negativity to one of abundance.

It's human nature to experience fear and anxiety. However, when you have faith, you realize that those emotions are there to encourage you to take action, not to hold you back. You can take a deep breath, control your emotions, and then shift your focus and turn fear into action. Face your fears by creating goals that are connected to your overall purpose in life. Setting and achieving goals that help you overcome your fears will give you a sense of accomplishment. Your goals don't have to be huge right away; taking small steps that add up to big results will improve your confidence and boost your ability to have faith in yourself.

If you're struggling to develop self-belief, you're likely focused on mistakes you've made in the past. When we learn from mistakes, we improve our performance on tasks we complete after making them. This is called having a growth mindset, and it's essential to believe in yourself. When you know that you can learn from your mistakes, you're much more willing to make them.

One way to begin developing a growth mindset is to challenge yourself to learn new things. Whether you learn how to write or play a guitar, acquiring a new skill can increase your feelings of self-efficacy, and your belief in your abilities to execute tasks, control your behavior, and attain your goals. Research has even shown that learning is directly related to happiness, as it releases dopamine in the brain, known as the "reward molecule." Learning enables you to form new neural connections, strengthen your decision-making skills, and more. By acquiring new skills, you'll begin to have faith in yourself, one step at a time.

Self-belief is about finding your inner strength so that you can embrace the journey that is life, with all its ups and downs, and realize that each challenge brings new skills, understanding, and strength. We all have times when we just don't think we can do it. The most important thing is to never give up. You'll inevitably encounter obstacles, but it's how you react to them that matters. Believing in yourself is all about digging deep and realigning your focus on what you want in life: discovering how to believe in yourself. It truly is within your reach.

Since our actions mirror self-belief, several things happen in our brains. It makes us become go-getters and inspires us to see the world of possibilities and the abundance of life. It is like reaping rewards and claiming what's rightly ours. In your mind, the moment you set your mind to it, it's yours. (Isn't it wonderful?)

We know we can't control everything that happens to us. But we also know there are many things we can do, such as focusing on ourselves. Life rewards us when we're proactive and concentrate on what we can do. Habit 1 by my favorite author of all time, Stephen Covey, in his book *7 Habits of Highly Effective People*, mentioned that being proactive is about taking responsibility for your life. You can't keep blaming everything on everyone around you. Proactive people recognize that they are responsible for their actions. They don't blame genetics, circumstances, conditions, or conditioning for their behavior. They know they choose their behavior. On the other hand, reactive people are often influenced by their physical environment. They tend to find external sources to blame for their behavior, claiming that someone else made them do it. Reactive people often let their physical environment dictate their feelings and behavior. If the weather is good, they feel good; if it's not, it affects their attitude and performance, and they blame the weather.

All of these external forces act as stimuli to which we respond. Between the stimulus and the response lies your greatest power: the freedom to choose your response. One of the most important things you choose is what you say. Your language is a good indicator of how you see yourself. A proactive person uses proactive language such as "I can," "I will," "I prefer," etc. Reactive people believe they are not responsible for what they say and do; they have no choice.

Proactive people focus their efforts on their Circle of Influence. They work on things they can do something about, such as their health, children, or problems at work.

Reactive people, on the other hand, focus their efforts on the Circle of Concern, which include things over which they have little or no control, like the national debt, terrorism, or the weather. Gaining awareness of the areas in which we expend our energies is a significant step in becoming proactive.

The magic happens simply by believing it's possible. Your belief in possibility is necessary for the work, experimentation, and consistency needed to change your life.

This belief in possibility is what provided rock stars with the single-minded intensity to get on stage every night, in the face of ridiculous odds. It's what gave famous authors the tenacity to keep writing and editing after countless rejected manuscripts. It's what kept star athletes training through pain, injury, and loss until they made it to the top. Now, you have some tools to start believing in yourself. Work on these steps consistently, and you will begin to see amazing things happening in your life.

A fantastic step to take in building your self-confidence and believing in yourself is setting and achieving goals. I encourage you never to compromise your integrity by trying to be, say, or feel something that is not true for you. And, more importantly, never compromise your potential to grow due to self-limiting doubts. Instead, embrace your confidence and believe in yourself because you really can achieve anything you put your mind to.

Chapter 13: Things you don't know about yourself

Your "self" lies before you like an open book. Just peer inside and read: who you are, your likes and dislikes, your hopes and fears; they are all there, ready to be understood. This notion is popular, but it also shows that we do not have privileged access to who we are. When we try to assess ourselves accurately, we are poking around in a fog.

I have read an interesting article where Princeton University psychologist Emily Pronin, who specializes in human self-perception and decision-making, calls the mistaken belief in privileged access the "introspection illusion." The way we view ourselves is distorted, but we do not realize it. As a result, our self-image has surprisingly little to do with our actions. For example, we may be convinced that we are empathetic and generous but still walk right past a homeless person on a cold day.

The reason for this distorted view is quite simple. Because we do not want to be stingy, arrogant, or self-righteous, we assume that we are not any of those things. Our brain is trying to protect us from the reality that we may not like. As evidence, she points to our divergent views of ourselves and others. We have no trouble recognizing how prejudiced or unfair our office colleague acts towards another person. But we do not consider that we could behave in much the same way: because we intend to be morally good, it never occurs to us that we, too, might be prejudiced.

Emily Pronin assessed her thesis through several experiments. Among other things, she had her study participants complete a test involving matching faces with personal statements that would supposedly assess their social intelligence. Afterward, some of them were told that they had failed and were asked to name weaknesses in the testing procedure. Although the opinions of the subjects were almost certainly biased (not only had they supposedly failed the test, but they were also being asked to critique it), most of the participants claimed that their evaluations were completely objective. This pattern was also evident in judging works of art, where subjects who used a biased strategy for assessing the quality of paintings nonetheless believed that their judgment was balanced. It may be possible that we are primed to mask our own biases.

Is the word "introspection" merely a nice metaphor? Could it be that we are not genuinely looking into ourselves or that we simply don't want to reveal much about ourselves, but instead, we are creating a flattering self-image that denies the flaws we all have? The research on self-knowledge has provided significant evidence for this conclusion. Despite thinking that we observe ourselves clearly, our self-image is influenced by unconscious processes.

How well do people truly know themselves? When attempting to answer this question, many researchers encounter the following problem: to assess a person's self-image, one would have to know who that person is. Investigators employ various techniques to address such questions. For instance, they compare the self-assessments of test subjects with their behavior in laboratory situations or everyday life.

To measure unconscious inclinations, psychologists can apply a method known as the implicit association test (iAT), developed in the 1990s by Anthony Greenwald of the University of Washington and his colleagues, to uncover hidden attitudes. Since then, numerous variants have been devised to examine anxiety, impulsiveness, and sociability among other features. The approach assumes that instantaneous reactions require no reflection; as a result, unconscious aspects of the personality come to the fore. Notably, experimenters seek to determine how closely words that are relevant to a person are linked to certain concepts.

Such "implicit" self-concepts generally correspond only weakly to assessments of the self. Psychologist Mitja Back of the University of Munster in Germany explains that methods designed to elicit automatic reactions reflect the spontaneous or habitual components of our personality. Conscientiousness and curiosity, on the other hand, require a certain amount of thought and can, therefore, be assessed more easily through self-reflection.

Much research indicates that our nearest and dearest often see us better than we see ourselves. Our self-assessments most closely match assessments by others when it comes to more neutral characteristics.

The characteristics that are generally most readable by others are those that strongly affect our behavior. For example, naturally sociable people typically like to talk and seek out company; insecurity often manifests in behaviors such as hand-wringing or averting one's gaze. In contrast, brooding is generally internal, unspooling within the confines of one's mind.

We are frequently blind to the effect we have on others because we simply do not see our own facial expressions, gestures, and body language. I am hardly aware that my blinking eyes indicate stress or that the slump in my posture betrays how heavily something weighs on me. Because it is so difficult to observe ourselves, we must rely on the observations of others, especially those who know us well. It is hard to know who we are unless others let us know how we affect them.

Gaining some distance can help you know yourself better. Keeping a diary, pausing for self-reflection, and having probing conversations with others have a long tradition, but whether these methods enable us to know ourselves is hard to tell. Sometimes doing the opposite, such as letting go, is more helpful because it provides some distance. I noticed how mindfulness meditation improves one's self-knowledge. It helps by overcoming two big hurdles: distorted thinking and ego protection. The practice of mindfulness teaches us to allow our thoughts to simply drift by and to identify with them as little as possible. Thoughts, after all, are "only thoughts" and not the absolute truth. Frequently, stepping out of oneself in this way and simply observing what the mind does fosters clarity. Gaining insight into our unconscious motives can enhance emotional well-being.

Our sense of well-being tends to grow as our conscious goals and unconscious motives become more aligned or congruent. For example, we should not slave away at a career that gives us money and power if these goals are of little importance to us. But how do we achieve such harmony? By imagining, for example. Try to imagine, as vividly and in as much detail as possible, how things would be if your most fervent wish came true. Would it make you happier? Often we succumb to the temptation to aim excessively high without taking into account all of the steps and efforts necessary to achieve ambitious goals.

We too often think we are better at something than we are. It holds that the more incompetent people are, the less they are aware of their incompetence. A general feature of self-perception: each of us tends to overlook our cognitive deficiencies.

So, why is the chasm between would-be and actual performance so gaping? Don't we all have an interest in assessing ourselves realistically? It surely would spare us a great deal of wasted effort and perhaps a few embarrassments. The answer, it seems, is that a moderate inflation of self-esteem has certain benefits.

People who tear themselves down experience setbacks more frequently. Although most of our contemporaries harbor excessively positive views of their honesty or intelligence, some people suffer from the opposite distortion: they belittle themselves and their efforts. Experiencing contempt and belittlement in childhood, often associated with violence and abuse, can trigger this kind of negativity which, in turn, can limit what people can accomplish, leading to distrust, and even suicidal thoughts.

It might seem logical to think that people with a negative self-image would be just the ones who would want to overcompensate. Yet, in an article I found, psychologists conducting a study at the University of Texas in Austin discovered that many individuals, plagued with self-doubt, seek confirmation of their distorted self-perception. The study focused on contentment in marriage, asking couples about their strengths and weaknesses, the ways they felt supported and valued by their partner, and how content they were in the marriage. As expected, those who had a more positive attitude toward themselves found greater satisfaction in their relationship the more they received praise and recognition from their partner. But those who habitually picked at themselves felt safer in their marriage when their partner reflected their negative image to them. They did not ask for respect or appreciation. On the contrary, they wanted to hear exactly their view of themselves: "You're incompetent." And no matter how hard the other partner tried to tell them otherwise, they were still unsatisfied, and in the end, one of them gave up.

Based on this theory of self-verification on these findings, it holds that we want others to see us the way we see ourselves. In some cases, people provoke others to respond negatively to them to prove how worthless they are. This behavior is not necessarily masochism. It is symptomatic of the desire for coherence. If others respond to us in a way that confirms our self-image, then the world is as it should be.

Likewise, people who consider themselves failures will go out of their way not to succeed, actively contributing to their undoing. They will miss meetings and habitually neglect doing assigned work.

You deceive yourself without realizing it. Our tendency for self-deception stems from our desire to impress others. To appear convincing, we must be convinced of our capabilities and truthfulness. Good salespeople, for example, exude a contagious enthusiasm; conversely, those who doubt themselves generally are not good at sweet talking. Our self-deceptions are quite changeable. Often we adapt them flexibly to new situations. Most people are somewhat embarrassed to hear their voices and can't stay alone with themselves. Although improvement and change are part of the normal maturation process, it feels good to believe that over time, one has become "who one is." Assuming that we have a solid code of identity reduces the complexity of a world that is constantly in flux. The people around us play many different roles, acting inconsistently and, at the same time, continuing to develop. It is reassuring to think that our friends will be precisely the same tomorrow as they are today and that they are good people, regardless of whether that perception is correct.

Insecure people tend to behave more morally. Insecurity is generally thought of as a drawback, but it is not entirely bad. People who feel insecure about whether they have some positive trait tend to try to prove that they do have it. Those who are unsure of their generosity, for example, are more likely to donate money to a good cause. This behavior can be elicited experimentally by giving subjects negative feedback. People dislike hearing such judgments and end up feeding the donation box.

So, what a particular action says about me is often more important than the action's actual objective. More than a few people have stuck with a diet because they did not want to appear weak-willed. Conversely, it has been empirically established that those who are sure that they are generous, intelligent, or sociable make less effort to prove it. Too much self-assurance makes people complacent and increases the chasm between the self that they imagine and the self that is real. Therefore, those who think they know themselves well are particularly apt to know themselves less well than they think.

When you think of yourself as flexible, you will do much better. People's theories about who they are influence how they behave. One's self-image can, therefore, easily become a self-fulfilling prophecy. If we view a characteristic as mutable, we are inclined to work on it more. On the other hand, if we view a trait such as IQ or willpower as largely unchangeable and inherent, we will do little to improve it. I observed that people with a rigid sense of self take failure badly. They see it as evidence of their limitations and fear it; fear of failure, meanwhile, can itself cause failure. In contrast, those who understand that a particular talent can be developed accept setbacks as an invitation to do better next time. This recommends an attitude aimed at personal growth. When in doubt, we should assume that we have something more to learn and that we can improve and develop. Even when our rigid sense of self is not fixed in all aspects of our personality, and even when we describe our strengths as completely stable, we tend to believe that we will outgrow our weaknesses sooner or later. If we try to imagine how our personality will look in several years, we lean toward views such as: "Level-headedness and clear focus will still be part and parcel of who I am, and I'll probably have fewer self-doubts."

Overall, we tend to view our character as more steadfast than it is, presumable because this assessment offers security and direction. We want to recognize our particular traits and preferences so that we can act accordingly. In the final analysis, the image that we create of ourselves is a kind of haven in an ever-changing world.

It has become clear that the self is not a "thing" but rather a process of continual adaptation to changing circumstances. And the fact that we so often see ourselves as more competent, moral, and stable than we are, serves our ability to adapt.

Chapter 14: Plan for your future self

What is my future? This question is a profound one: those of us who wonder about our future exhibit an especially healthy form of curiosity that augurs greater well-being over time.

Once upon a time, we were our past selves. We moved forward with either future intentions in mind or simply drifted with the tide. Did we ever think that we would have ended up where we are?

Few people I know expected to be exactly where they are today. So how can we plan for our futures when they are so uncertain?

The answer is not to focus solely on what we want or what we want to be in the future, but rather, on who we want to be and how we picture ourselves becoming.

After all, in life, the only person we can truly depend on is ourselves. As much as we may wish to rely on someone else wholeheartedly, sometimes they leave, change, or even pass away.

Who you are in the future depends on what you do today. One of the problems we humans can encounter when setting and reaching our goals is that we envision ourselves as the person we are right now, rather than the person we will become when we achieve those goals. We haven't fully connected with that future version of ourselves. However, research shows that when we establish a stronger connection to that future version of ourselves, we are more likely to take actions now that will benefit the person we will eventually become– whether it's 30 minutes or 30 years from now.

This past year, I started visualizing the future that I wanted. Before then, I had no idea what I desired or how I pictured my future. By becoming more visual about my aspirations, I truly connected with my future and now feel confident in the steps I need to take to achieve the life I desire. I allowed myself to contemplate my desires while having fun doing it, making the process feel less overwhelming and more enjoyable as I visually mapped out my life.

For all of us daydreamers, creating a visual plan for our lives can add a practical dimension to our daydreams. With the right approach, we can be daydreamers with real, actionable plans for our future.

Before delving into all of this, I want to emphasize some important points about my approach to visual planning. These are things we all know, but it's essential to remind ourselves of them while mapping out our futures visually.

I understand that creating a roadmap for the future does not guarantee that things will unfold exactly as envisioned. Life is full of unexpected and unplanned events, and that's part of its beauty. Nonetheless, I don't see any harm in having a vision for my future. There is value in aspiring for things, even if reality deviates from the exact vision. Moreover, we have the freedom to change our minds about our future plans over and over again, and that's perfectly okay!

In my visualization of the future, there are some physical belongings that I would like to possess someday. However, I think these are the least important aspects when it comes to the future. The most important factor to me is to be happy and fulfilled in life with the people I love next to me. Nonetheless, I think it's acceptable to work towards acquiring physical possessions, as long as we don't attach excessive importance to them. Ultimately, belongings are just material things, and it's the relationships we build that hold the greatest value.

I firmly believe that achieving requires hard work and trust in our vision for ourselves. Merely visualizing without taking action won't lead to success. It's essential to invest energy and effort into making those visions a reality. Mapping it out can help point you in the right direction. It can encourage you and show you the way, but it can't and won't do the work for you.

We can all daydream about having mansions all across the country. A beach house in California, a fabulous apartment in New York City, and a getaway house in Europe. We can pin these dreams on Pinterest without any intention of ever pursuing them. There's nothing wrong with that, but if your other goals don't align with that extravagant future, I don't see the point. Instead, consider daydreaming about things that are a little more realistic yet equally amazing. Daydream about your Paris trip while you're studying your French and putting money away into an account every month. The person who is doing that is way more interesting to me than the one who hasn't taken steps toward their outlandish daydream. (PS: I'm 100% guilty of being that girl I'm complaining about at times, but sometimes I just need a little push to start working towards my own goals and aspirations.)

This year, I set three large goals for myself: To move out of my parent's house, to finish my book and publish it, and to get a real estate license (which I just achieved!) These are significant changes that align with my vision for myself. I didn't go overboard with all the things. (Okay, that's a lie. I have my apartment's color scheme and everything all planned out before I've even found an apartment.) But I focused on my big three goals before diving into other details. While there are many things I want, I believe it's important to prioritize the most significant ones that bring me closer to my goals. Other things may fall into place without me even realizing it. I suggest starting small with the most important priorities and building from there.

Here's why it's helpful to get visual and plan out your future:
1. You constantly ask yourself what you want and what is important to you.
2. You constantly realize what you don't want and what is not important to you.
3. You're more likely to figure out how to get there because you know where you want to go.
4. You can visually see yourself achieving your goals.
5. You can feel when you're not on the right path.

6. You can confidently turn down opportunities that don't serve you.
7. You can seek guidance from those who have already accomplished what you aim to do.

Focus on how you want to feel before you think about what you physically want to have. Remind yourself why you want what you do in life. Why does it matter to you? Why do you care about this?

Your "why's" are important, so hold onto them. Businesses use mission statements to guide everything they do as a company. If it doesn't align with the mission, it has no place in their business plan. The same should apply to you and your life. Setting your mission statement will make it much easier to visualize your future. You can ask yourself, "Does this fit my mission?" before proceeding with a decision.

When you're evaluating what is most important, explore every aspect of your life and contemplate how you'd like to feel and what you envision.

Here is a list of some of the areas of life I think about:
- Home
- Friendships
- Romantic Relationships
- Family
- Career
- Travel
- Car-Transportation
- Health
- Community
- Hobbies
- Fashion, and so on.

What do you see there? What does the ideal version of you do? What are you driving? What are you wearing? What are you working on? Where do you live? Do you have kids? Do you own a business? How often do you travel?

The more you explore this with a realistic and open mind, the closer you get to working on getting where you want to be. There are a variety of ways in which you can do it. For example: writing a letter to your future self. You might hear this advice many times from multiple sources, but this is an effective way to picture yourself where you want to go and be. This is a significant step towards becoming more visual. I wrote a letter to myself as if I was addressing my future self-three years later. I discussed my accomplishments and what I am doing. I went through the list of life categories (listed above) and expressed how proud I was of the life I had built for myself. It opened my eyes a lot. I will be 35 in a few years, and during that time, many life-changing things can happen, and I want them to happen. Writing about the life you desire to have in a few years instills the mindset to start working towards making those dreams a reality.

I'm new to mind mapping, but I think it sounds so fun and helpful. I typically see mind maps as study tools, but they can also be used to provide a clearer and more visual perspective for your future. They help you get specific and guide you on the actions needed to reach your desired destination. You can add more details later on after constructing a mind map. Consider what steps you can take to achieve your visions and goals. It's truly a great way to organize your thoughts in a visually pleasing way.

Mind map ideas:
1. Your big-picture goals: What do you hope to accomplish this year?
2. Your priorities: What is important to you, and what can you do to improve it?
3. Specific ideas: For your business, blog, or personal life.

Use Pinterest realistically. Instead of pinning boards with no intention but to daydream, start pinning with purpose. If you're moving house, look for pins that will guide you along the way. If you're looking to enhance your wardrobe, search for outfit ideas to inspire your choices before buying new items. It might even help you with what you already own. Focus on finding inspiration for the near future rather than the distant and unlikely future.

Similar to Pinterest, a vision board provides a source of inspiration. Cut out pictures from magazines that you feel represent who you want to be and what you want to feel. Vision boards can be a great way to visually remind yourself of what you want to accomplish. Seeing it every day can be truly motivating. Choose words that hold meaning for you. Be selective with your vision board and change it up as you see fit.

Let's get visual! Let us know how you like to plan visually. Have you tried any of these methods before? Did they make an impact on your future steps? Did they move you closer to your goals and your vision of your future self? …that made me wonder, as a researcher, what kinds of things your future self will thank you for?

There are times when you might want to be a little discreet, but there are two very good reasons why you should communicate your plans: so that you know what you are doing, and others know what you are doing.

I don't mean to suggest that you don't know what you are doing, but having a clear plan to communicate to others means you will have a much clearer sense of your priorities: why you have decided to do something (and not something else) when you will do the things you need to do, who else needs to be involved, and perhaps even a sense of how you are going to do things. If you have a clear plan, then you have a strong foundation for effective communication.

I think we've all experienced moments when someone else's plans, usually someone we felt we could not say 'no' to, impinged on or ruined our plans, and these are most infuriating or frustrating when this happens at the last minute.

Then, I realized that communication of my plans was limited: it mostly consisted of telling others what plans entailed, with little detail beyond the immediate week or two. It rarely included the reasons behind my plans, nor did it involve listening to others' plans, so that appropriate actions could be negotiated, accommodated, and workloads fairly managed. This extended beyond the workplace to home life, including household chores.

Telling others your plans can also represent a psychological commitment (perhaps why we don't verbalize them). However, by not sharing our plans, we are less likely to commit to them, and just as importantly, we miss out on valuable advice and support. This might be why we refrain from verbalizing them; sometimes, the responses from others can be off-putting. I often feel a bit embarrassed about sharing my long-term ambitions or plans. I fear being scoffed at or seen as "thinking too highly of myself." Yet, I have come to realize that having goals, even ambitious ones, is not immodest. And far from scoffing, there are a lot of people who want to see you succeed and are prepared to help, or at least accommodate. You don't have to broadcast your plans to the world, but letting it be known to enablers that you'd love to work on X or would be open to an invitation to collaborate on Y means that others will think of you when those opportunities arise. Your future self can thank these 'enabler' people when you get tipped off about your dream job, but your future self can also thank your past self for communicating in the first place.

Acknowledgments

There are countless people I would like to thank for their help throughout my life, without whom I would not be who I am or doing what I do. For the sake of brevity here, I would like to acknowledge and thank those who have had the greatest impact on the success of this book.

First, I want to thank those of you who have read this book and made it so far. I hope you found this book interesting and valuable as much as it was for me when I wrote it.

Thank you, Mom, Brother, and all my family members and friends. Without their support, this book never would have come to be.

Thank you, Newton Lee, who has inspired me every day with his incredible thoughtfulness and his care for the people around him. Working with him in the past few years has been a blessing. He is a person I admire and look up to.

Thank you, the book editor Dr. Bilawal Shah for helping edit the book and giving constructive criticism in helping this book to be more structured and ready for the readers.

Bibliography

"Amy Cuddy: Your Body Languages Shapes Who You Are." TED: Ideas worth Spreading N.p.,n.d.Web. 12 Nov. 2013.
http://www.ted.com/talks/amy_cuddy_your_body_language_shapes_who_you_are.html

"Daniel Kahneman: The Riddle of Experience vs. Memory." TED: Ideas worth speeding. N.p., n.d. Web. 12 Nov. 2013.
https://www.ted.com/talks/daniel_kahneman_the_riddle_of_experience_vs_memory

Dennett, Daniel Clement. "Experience." Consciousness Explained. London U.a.: Lane, the Penguin, 1992 N. pag. Print.

Print Flynn, Thomas, Flynn, "Jean-Paul Satre." Stanford University. Stanford University, 22 Apr. 2004. Web. 13 Nov. 2013.
https://plato.stanford.edu/entries/sartre/

Grattan, Nikki, and Klea McKenna. "Maja Ruznic." In the Make N.p., Oct. 2012 Web. 6 Nov 2013. http://inthemake.com/maja-ruznic/

"Hetain Patel: Who Am I? Think Again." Ted: Ideas worth Spreading. N.p., n.d. Web. 12 Nov. 2013.
https://www.ted.com/talks/hetain_patel_who_am_i_think_again

"Julian Baggini: Is There a Real You?" TED: Ideas worth Spreading. N.p., Web. 12 Nov. 2013. https://www.ted.com/talks/julian_baggini_is_there_a_real_you

Mitchell Stephen A., and Margaret J. Black, Freud and Beyond: A History of Modern Psychoanalytic Thought. New York: Basic, 1995 Print.

Pickover, Clifford A. Time: A Traveler's Guide. New York 1998 Print.
"Radiolab." Idea Explorer. N.p., n.d. Web. 12 Nov. 2013.
https://www.wnycstudios.org/story/91569-memory-and-forgetting

"Radiolab." Radiolab Podcast Articles. N.p., n.d. Web 12 Nov. 2013.
https://www.wnycstudios.org/story/259774-solid-rock

Ronnberg, Ami, and Kathleen Martin. The Book of Symbols, Koln: Taschen, 2010. Print.

"Ruby Wax: What's so Funny about Mental Illness?" TED: Ideas worth Spreading. N.p., n.d. Web. 12 Nov. 2013.
https://www.ted.com/talks/ruby_wax_what_s_so_funny_about_mental_illness

Shoemaker, David, Shoemaker, "Personal Identity and Ethics." Stanford University. 20 Dec. 2005. Web. 13 Nov. 2013.
https://plato.stanford.edu/entries/identity-ethics/

Simon, Hilda. Color in Reproduction: Theory and Techniques for Artists and Designers. New York: Viking 1980 Print.

"Global Awareness" N.p., n.d. Web 9 Dec. 2011.
https://www.globalawareness.com/2011/12/the importance-of-cultural-exchange/

"Mental Health" N.p., Web 2015. https://www.mentalhelp.net/understanding-your-problem/self-identity

"Conver Company" N.p., n.d. Web 26 Jan. 2018
https://www.conovercompany.com/self-esteem-outside-influences/

"Medical News Today" N.p., n.d. Web 9 Jun. 2020
https://www.medicalnewstoday.com/articles/introvert-definition

"Very Well Mind" N.p., n.d.Web 12 Aug. 2020
https://www.verywellmind.com/what-is-personality-2795416
Know Thyself: To Awaken Self-Realization by Lateef Terrell Warnick's book

"Self-understanding" N.p., n.d. Web 21 July 2021
https://www.lifehack.org/682908/how-to-attain-self-realization-a-guide-to-become-a-better-you

"Toxic Relationships" N.p., n.d. Web 3 Oct 2020
https://www.psychologytoday.com/intl/blog/toxic-relationships/202010/how-we-lose-ourselves-in-relationships

"21 examples of healthy boundaries in relationships" N.p., n.d. Web 31 May 2021 https://liveboldandbloom.com/05/relationships/healthy-boundaries-in-relationships

"Iulian Ionescu" N.p., n.d. Web 8 Sept 2021
https://iulianionescu.com/blog/how-our-beliefs-and-values-shape-our-behavior/

"Cyntia Bazin" N.p., n.d. Web 14 Jan 2016 https://www.success.com/5-qualities-you-need-to-reach-your-biggest-goals/

"Amy Morin" N.p., n.d. Web 12 July 2017 https://www.success.com/13-things-mentally-strong-people-dont-do/

www.ingramcontent.com/pod-product-compliance
Lightning Source LLC
Chambersburg PA
CBHW060832050426
42453CB00008B/658